"The Object Lessons series achieves something very close to magic: the books take ordinary—even banal—objects and animate them with a rich history of invention, political struggle, science, and popular mythology. Filled with fascinating details and conveyed in sharp, accessible prose, the books make the everyday world come to life. Be warned: once you've read a few of these, you'll start walking around your house, picking up random objects, and musing aloud: 'I wonder what the story is behind this thing?'"

Steven Johnson, author of *Where Good Ideas Come From* and *How We Got to Now*

"Object Lessons describe themselves as 'short, beautiful books,' and to that, I'll say, amen. . . . If you read enough Object Lessons books, you'll fill your head with plenty of trivia to amaze and annoy your friends and loved ones—caution recommended on pontificating on the objects surrounding you. More importantly, though . . . they inspire us to take a second look at parts of the everyday that we've taken for granted. These are not so much lessons about the objects themselves, but opportunities for self-reflection and storytelling. They remind us that we are surrounded by a wondrous world, as long as we care to look."

John Warner, *The Chicago Tribune*

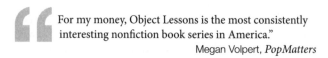

For my money, Object Lessons is the most consistently interesting nonfiction book series in America."

Megan Volpert, *PopMatters*

Besides being beautiful little hand-sized objects themselves, showcasing exceptional writing, the wonder of these books is that they exist at all. . . . Uniformly excellent, engaging, thought-provoking, and informative."

Jennifer Bort Yacovissi,
Washington Independent Review of Books

. . . edifying and entertaining . . . perfect for slipping in a pocket and pulling out when life is on hold."

Sarah Murdoch, *Toronto Star*

[W]itty, thought-provoking, and poetic. . . . These little books are a page-flipper's dream."

John Timpane, *The Philadelphia Inquirer*

Though short, at roughly 25,000 words apiece, these books are anything but slight."

Marina Benjamin, *New Statesman*

OBJECTLESSONS

A book series about the hidden lives of ordinary things.

Series Editors:

Ian Bogost and Christopher Schaberg

Advisory Board:

Sara Ahmed, Jane Bennett, Jeffrey Jerome Cohen, Johanna Drucker, Raiford Guins, Graham Harman, renée hoogland, Pam Houston, Eileen Joy, Douglas Kahn, Daniel Miller, Esther Milne, Timothy Morton, Kathleen Stewart, Nigel Thrift, Rob Walker, Michele White.

In association with

 Georgia ∥ Center for Tech ∥ Media Studies

BOOKS IN THE SERIES

political sign

TOBIAS CARROLL

BLOOMSBURY ACADEMIC
NEW YORK • LONDON • OXFORD • NEW DELHI • SYDNEY

BLOOMSBURY ACADEMIC
Bloomsbury Publishing Inc
1385 Broadway, New York, NY 10018, USA
50 Bedford Square, London, WC1B 3DP, UK

BLOOMSBURY, BLOOMSBURY ACADEMIC and the Diana logo are trademarks of
Bloomsbury Publishing Plc

First published in the United States of America 2020

Cover design: Alice Marwick

Bloomsbury Publishing Inc does not have any control over, or responsibility for, any third-
party websites referred to or in this book. All internet addresses given in this book were
correct at the time of going to press. The author and publisher regret any inconvenience
caused if addresses have changed or sites have ceased
to exist, but can accept no responsibility for any such changes.

Library of Congress Cataloging-in-Publication Data
Names: Carroll, Tobias, author.
Title: Political sign / Tobias Carroll.
Description: New York, NY: Bloomsbury Academic, 2020. |
Series: Object lessons | Includes bibliographical references and index.
Identifiers: LCCN 2020013062 | ISBN 9781501358104 (paperback) |
ISBN 9781501358128 (pdf) | ISBN 9781501358111 (ebook)
Subjects: LCSH: Political participation–Social aspects–United States. | Advertising,
Political–United States. | Signs and signboards–Political aspects–United States. |
Party affiliation–Social aspects–United States.
Classification: LCC JK1764 .C36 2020 | DDC 306.20973–dc23
LC record available at https://lccn.loc.gov/2020013062

ISBN: PB: 978-1-5013-5810-4
ePDF: 978-1-5013-5812-8
eBook: 978-1-5013-5811-1

Series: Object Lessons

Typeset by Deanta Global Publishing Services, Chennai, India
Printed and bound in Great Britain

To find out more about our authors and books visit www.bloomsbury.com
and sign up for our newsletters.

For my parents

CONTENTS

INTRODUCTION

If you grew up anywhere in the United States where there was open space, you probably saw them punctuating the local lawns and median strips and vacant lots in the weeks leading up to Election Day. Halloween decorations beside squat rectangular placards pounded into the surface of the earth. In retrospect, their ubiquity borders on the comic. Where else can a sign advertising a home for sale, a sign touting the services of a lawn care company, and a sign endorsing a candidate for the highest office in the land all take on the same proportions, the same placement, the same significance?

It isn't hard to see political signs wherever you look. They might be touting candidates running in a general election or for their party's nomination in a primary. They might be held aloft as a gesture of protest, or as part of a counterprotest. You might even see one rendered as a tattoo on someone's body, or transformed into a work of art hanging in a museum. You can see them in the background of historical photos or contained within coffee-table books, lurking in the background of film and television sets, or at the corners of a comic book panel.

And if you see enough of them, when you know what to look for, you can start to read places like books: the inner workings and deeply held beliefs of towns or cities or counties, all ready to be revealed.

*   *   *

This is a book about political signs. As such, it's covering a lot of territory. The little signs hawking a particular candidate that dot suburban lawns in the autumn months? Political sign. The handwritten poster held aloft at a protest to challenge the status quo? Political sign. The billboard set up beside a highway by one political party or advocacy group? Political sign. The nineteenth-century illustration of a presidential candidate as a hardy blacksmith? That's a political sign as well.

But political signs can go beyond that. In 2012, a man got a face tattoo of the logo of Republican presidential nominee Mitt Romney,[1] effectively transforming himself into a walking political sign. The use of political signage in sports, whether on the field or in the stands, remains hotly debated and varies dramatically from league to league and sport to sport. And certain political signs have gone on to have an unexpected afterlife in museums or as props on stage and screen. What does a political sign mean outside of an explicitly political context? Does that context defang it, or does it subtly transform the surrounding space?

Consider this book a kind of mixtape, blending case studies with personal reflection and a few forays into theory. In recent years, political signage has undergone a series of convulsions and transformations, with the presidential campaigns of Barack Obama in 2008 and Donald Trump in 2016 using signage in fascinating and even transformative ways. The same could be said for the "Leave" campaign in the United Kingdom in the summer of 2016—and a host of other elections and referendums around the globe.

Some political signs are universal, while others are specific to their time, place, or region. But all of them can tell us something about the circumstances under which they were made, from the most generic ones imaginable to something hyper-targeted to a specific audience. Consider it something that comes with the printed nature of the signs. "Print gave intensity and uniform precision, where before there had been a diffuse texture," wrote Marshall McLuhan in his book *Understanding Media*. "Print brought in the taste for exact measurement and repeatability that we now associate with science and mathematics."[2]

Every political sign tells a story. It may not be a particularly complex or pleasant one, but it's a story regardless. When I spoke with Susan Carlson, Assistant Curator at the International Center of Photography, she talked about the motifs that recur in political campaigns. "Themes, imagery, and catchphrases are all repeated frequently," Carlson said. "For example, Republicans used Ronald Reagan's 'Win one for the Gipper' in various ways in the campaigns for not only Reagan, but also George H. W. Bush, Bob Dole, and George

W. Bush." Political signs and other ephemera, it could be argued, were memes before the term was ubiquitous.

*   *   *

In 1992, Buena Vista Pictures released a comedy starring Eddie Murphy called *The Distinguished Gentleman*. It is, I think it's fair to say, no one's favorite Eddie Murphy vehicle— it came at the point in his career, encountered by many comedians, where the precision and energy of his early work was softened somewhat for a new role as a matinee idol. The plotline does indeed involve helping sick children, and there are plenty of elements of it that feel paint-by-numbers. I can remember watching it on a plane flying home from visiting Florida. I can remember all of one joke, as well as the fact that the actor who played Miles Silverberg on the television show *Murphy Brown* was in the cast.

But the central idea of *The Distinguished Gentleman* was actually utterly brilliant, and in an era where nearly everything from the 1970s through the 1990s has been remade, rebooted, or reiterated, I'm almost shocked to see that no one else has picked up its central conceit and run with it.

Here's the premise: Murphy plays a man named Thomas Jefferson Johnson. His representative in Congress is a man named Jeff Johnson, whose death sets the film's plot into motion. Murphy's character runs for the vacant office using his middle name and last name, figuring that it's a way to become rich and famous. But it's a cynical move, based on the assumption that the residents of his area will vote him into office based on nothing but name recognition. Of course, it works—and, for the rest of the film, audiences are treated to a civics lesson starring Eddie Murphy, which is as strange as it sounds.

A look at the credited screenwriters for *The Distinguished Gentleman* reveals one particularly interesting name. That would be one Marty Kaplan, whose career as a writer began in the Jimmy Carter administration. There, he was Walter Mondale's chief speechwriter; he would later serve as the deputy campaign manager for Mondale's presidential run in 1984.[3] All of which is to say: the central concept at the heart of *The Distinguished Gentleman* is that name recognition can go a long way in politics—and the person making that argument has a wealth of experience in that particular arena.

Name recognition counts for a lot. What's generally the largest thing on any political sign for a particular campaign? The candidate's last name. Think of Jeb Bush's generally underwhelming 2016 run for the Republican presidential nomination—one which put his first name, rather than his last name, front and center. Were there other reasons for that? Sure: His brother George's presidency is not terribly well-remembered, and there's a question to be made of whether or not that name recognition would have hurt rather than helped him.

Arguably, the 2016 election could be held up as a litmus test for just how much name recognition matters; see also, Hilary Clinton's presidential campaign. Names on a sign can tell a story as much as signs themselves can.

* * *

You can read a place through the signs you see there. You can find evidence of political beliefs or challenge conventional wisdom. You can see protests in action, see truth spoken to power. This is a book about signs, a book about reading, and a book about how one thing becomes another. In the end, it's a book about stories: the stories political signs tell, the stories we tell ourselves about them, and the stories they become after time has passed. Listen.

1 THE UBIQUITY OF YARD SIGNS

There's something eminently tactile about yard signs—the legs, for one thing, which can be hammered into the earth of a front yard or median strip or vacant lot. Their height, suitable for tripping or other awkward collisions made while navigating through suburban neighborhoods long after twilight. The accumulated dirt and grime that clings to their exteriors after a rainy spell, and the act of washing them down or wiping them off to keep them looking sharp right up until the election.

And then there's the final removal of signage, whether in the aftermath of an election or long past it. Perhaps your candidate of choice emerged victorious and you feel a sense of relief as you pull it up. *Finally*, you think. *This is done. We did it.* Maybe your feelings are more ambivalent. Maybe your chosen candidate came up short. Maybe you decide to keep it in place for just a little longer, to show the world who you are or what you believe in.

Or maybe not. And there you are in the early days of November, your skin touching the cold metal frame of the yard sign, reminding you of the change of seasons. Call it a lesson, perhaps. Call it something.

*   *   *

Political signs taught me a lesson once, though it wasn't the one I was hoping for.

I grew up in Monmouth County, New Jersey. It's about an hour south of New York and ninety minutes east of Philadelphia. It's Bruce Springsteen and Kevin Smith territory; it has archetypal postwar suburbs like the neighborhood where I grew up, but it also has great live music venues, interesting theater, and some of my favorite places in the world.

I was born two days before the American people went to the polls, voted Jimmy Carter into office, and in doing so brought Gerald Ford's time in the White House to a close. Being a newborn, I was utterly unaware of any of this. I have no memories of either the Ford or Carter administrations. While both of them have strong political beliefs, neither of my parents has ever registered as a member of a political party. This led to a general avoidance of politics, or at least partisan politics, being discussed around the house when I was growing up.

My first awareness of political candidates as such came when I was seven: I remember one of my classmates talking about his certainty that one of the men running for office in 1984 would lead the nation into a nuclear war. I don't remember if it was Ronald Reagan or Walter Mondale who was the target of his fear, to be honest, and in retrospect I'm reasonably sure that he was repeating opinions he'd heard from parents or older siblings. Still, there it was: my first creaking awareness that the votes our parents were casting, and that we would eventually cast, had consequences.

There's a degree of privilege involved in that, of course, and a degree of isolation. If I was writing a novel about a seven-year-old, I'd almost certainly give them at least a cursory awareness of these aspects of the world. But my own life is not the result of a narrative I wrote, and so I can only look back on my earlier actions and beliefs and sigh.

The other element of my blind spots relative to politics growing up had to do with the time in which I grew up. By which I mean, for most of my childhood the Cold War was still in full swing, and the threat of nuclear war felt very real. As a child, I remember having the certainty that a nuclear war would be what did me in—though that was admittedly at a time when my awareness of my own mortality was blessedly incomplete. But that might have been a factor in my ignorance of politicians and factions: If the world as we knew it was about to end, why bother learning about the difference between Republicans and Democrats?

* * *

That younger version of me didn't know much about political parties or candidates for office, but he was certainly aware of elections themselves. Every year in early November, my parents would hop in the car and drive a few minutes down Hance Avenue, to the local polling site located within the Monmouth Church of Christ. I knew very little about this church—I was raised Episcopalian, and the church I grew up attending was a little further down the road, one town away—save that a few of my classmates went there with their families.

It was a nondescript room with a few voting machines: the metal industrial kind with tabs to be flipped down beside your candidate of choice and a massive lever to throw when you were ready to finalize your vote. I have dim memories of going into the booth with one of my parents when I was very young. I also have memories of being handed some sort of kid-sized version of the voting machine to play with and, assumably, learn how representative democracy worked. At some point, I became too old to go into the voting booth or play with the miniature ballot, and I lingered until my parents voted. Soon, I was old enough to stay home when they trekked out to cast their votes. My next time back in the Monmouth Church of Christ was on Election Day 1994, when I cast my first vote there.

At some point before then, I began to make the connection between the signs I'd see all over people's lawns in the lead-up to the election—and sometimes for weeks afterward—and the curtained chamber in a temporary facility where my parents and their peers would vote, and where I would someday vote as well.

* * *

I haven't lived in Monmouth County for twenty years, but I'm back to visit a lot. I still have plenty of friends and family there; several of them have dogs, and I'm not immune to the lure of quality time with a friendly beagle. Between birthdays and holidays, I'm back there pretty frequently in the latter quarter of the year. And so there I was in the fall of 2018, driving around near the town where I grew up and the town where my parents now live. Nearly everywhere I went, I saw signs with the name "Hugin" emblazoned on them. I saw them on lawns, on stray bits of unclaimed grass, on the side of a lot as I crossed the Swimming River on Route 520.

"Hugin" in this case was one Bob Hugin, the Republican challenging Democratic senator Robert Menendez for his seat in that year's election. Menendez won that election—most of the candidates New Jersey has elected to statewide office in the last twenty years have been Democrats—but the density of Hugin signs around where I grew up served as a pretty solid indicator of the region's politics.

Shortly after the 2016 presidential election, writer Melissa Febos wrote about her classroom experiences teaching at Monmouth University in the waning months of the year for the journal *Granta*. Her essay, "Teaching After Trump," resonated with me deeply for a host of reasons. Predominant among them was the fascinating experience of reading a writer who grew up elsewhere, and whose work I admire tremendously, chronicle a region I thought I knew well.

I work, however, in a red county in New Jersey, at a private university where Trump was elected by a small margin in our undergraduate student body's straw poll. Our students are more than 60 per cent white, with a high number of first generation college students. Despite it being an hour's drive away, many of them have never been to Manhattan. Most of them have never left the country, and some not even the county—for lack of motivation rather than resources.[1]

Reading this hit me like a revelation. Two years later, seeing the omnipresent signs extolling Robert Hugin's candidacy, I was reminded of it. But I also realized something: I might have been able to make a similar assessment of the area, had I only paid attention to the literal signs around me.

2 THE SIGN WARS

Political signage can serve as a guidepost in space and time around the globe. Kathleen Jamie's essay collection *Sightlines* focuses on her experience with the natural world and with history in and around Scotland. But in one essay, "The Woman in the Field," she recalls a particular moment from her youth that's remained with her over the years. The year is 1979, and the natural landscape has been punctuated by something new, signifying a shift in her country's politics.

> Blue election posters were still nailed to roadside trees, but they would soon be removed. They'd done their work— ten days before, Margaret Thatcher had been voted into office.[1]

Jamie's inclusion of public space gets at another way that yard signs—and political signs in general—aren't simply confined to the yards of political enthusiasts or supporters of a particular candidate. In some locations, public spaces and liminal sites like open fields and the sides of highways are fair game, to say nothing of the source of endless controversy.

Right about now might be a good time to talk about the sign wars.

"The sign wars in Newark go back roughly to the 17th century, when the city was first settled by a small band of Puritans," wrote David Giambusso at the *The Star-Ledger* in 2014. "Indeed, the tradition of posting notices, treatises and declarations on public walls and trees is an American tradition."[2]

Giambusso's article looked at the tension between advocates for two opposing candidates for mayor in a citywide election in Newark. Ras Baraka and Shavar Jeffries each sought the office, which had been recently vacated after Cory Booker was elected to the Senate; the article focused on the frustrations experienced by residents of one particular Newark neighborhood. As Giambusso phrased it, "in the age of glossy ads and brightly colored campaign posters, the denizens of Forest Hill—a neighborhood of stately mansions and large, well-kept homes—say they have had enough."

New Jersey is a densely populated state with active and long-running party organizations in both the Democratic and Republican camps; that's one of several reasons why the distribution and posting of political signage there can seem like the stuff of high drama. But the frustrations of the residents of Forest Hill pale in comparison to some of the conflicts taking place in nearby Passaic County, which led to accusations of criminal activity— fraudulent criminal activity—and enough misdirection to power a dozen paranoid thrillers.

This was the scene, in the lead-up to a contentious race for Sheriff in a county-wide 2013 election. Writing in *The Record*, Zach Paterberg described the act that kicked a heap of accusations and counteractions into high gear.

> On Thursday, campaign staff for Sheriff Richard Berdnik, a Democrat who faces a stiff challenge from GOP challenger Frank Feenan next month, released four videos showing teams of people removing campaign signs of Berdnik and other Democratic office seekers from places such as the corner of McBride and Glover avenues in Woodland Park. The surveillance videos were shot by several cameras that campaign loyalists have trained on Berdnik posters because of the high number of thefts.[3]

The controversy didn't end there. Instead, members of Feenan's staff charged that the video was a fake—that someone associated with Berdnik's campaign had posed as a vandal in order to discredit their counterparts working for Feenan. It's worth mentioning that, as political scandals in New Jersey go, this is a relatively mild one. But it's also representative of the scrappiness that can sometimes emerge with respect to the state's elections.

Shortly after midnight on an October night in 2012, a man working for the Democratic Coordinating Campaign in New Jersey was arrested in the town of Mahwah. According to one news report, two police officers saw the man removing signs for two Republican freeholders' re-election campaign from a median strip on Route 17. The article notes that police "found eight more Hermansen-Watkins signs behind the drivers seat and a pile of re-elect Senator Menendez signs in the back of the car." The man's defense? He was doing it to counterbalance the theft of signs supporting the re-election of Democratic senator Robert Menendez.[4]

Whether partisan-minded or not, removal of political signs can sometimes have unanticipated consequences. In 2012, Keith Edwards of New Hampshire's *Kennebec Journal* wrote about a clash between politics and commerce playing out near Lakeside Orchards in Maine. Edwards writes that "political signs, including some signs against the ballot question for same-sex marriage, were put along the road on the orchard's property without the permission of anyone who works there."[5]

Lakeside Orchards' owner sought to keep politics out of the business, and the shop's manager took the signs down. That, too, hit a snag: Maine has laws on the books against removing political signs, if you weren't the person who initially set them up.

"Removing political signs when they're in allowed spaces is illegal under Maine law, punishable by a fine of up to $250. Allowed spots include within the state right of way along roads," Edwards noted. "Landowners can remove signs on their property, but not when it is within the state right of way."[6] Which in turn can create a headache for a business when someone assumes, based on the proximity of signs to their property, that they hold a political position that they actually don't.

In an article for *The Atlantic*, journalist Lane Wallace wrote about the abundance of yard signs she saw in her town of Marblehead, Massachusetts.

> As the days have ticked down to election day, the sprinkling of "Obama" and "Romney" signs has become a full-court-press flood of entire opposing team benches: Obama-Biden-Warren-Tierney vs. Romney-Ryan-Brown-Tisei. In many cases, those competing team rosters are planted squarely next to, or across the street from, each other, making me wonder if one side's signs didn't prompt the appearance of the other's.[7]

Wallace observes that her town's residents have avoided vandalizing or stealing signs, and offers some thoughts as to why this might be the case. This, in turn, leads her to ponder the signs' role in increasing discord in the local community. "I've found myself wondering less about the potential merits of either camp than about how all those neighbors are going to be able to get along, a week or so from now," she writes.[8] This led her to research whether or not signs actually make a difference in elections. Her conclusion is that they don't have much, if any, effect on the outcome; instead, the endurance of their presence on grassy surfaces across the United States is more a sign of polarization and "politics as sport"[9] than anything else.

Even so, there's still that question of name recognition, of a newfound familiarity with a candidate's name translating into a vote cast for that candidate. Is it too ephemeral to measure? Or is it simply, like so many things in life, a tradition that feels more effective than it actually is?

*　*　*

Sometimes, yard signs can prompt disagreements that go beyond simple arguments. In 2017, a pair of nineteen-year-old women were charged with a hate crime in Maryland for setting a pro–Donald Trump sign on fire. The context: the owner of a sporting goods store put up a sign reading "Trump: Make America Great Again" in front of his store in the fall of 2016. After the election, he left it up;[10] call it a victory lap, a statement of ideology, or just flat-out trolling.

The sign, in front of Wink's Sporting Goods in Princess Anne, certainly frustrated D'Asia R. Perry and Joy M. Shuford, who apparently decided to set it on fire. Their attempt at creative immolation didn't work, however; to make matters worse, Perry and Shuford soon found themselves charged with a host of offenses—including the aforementioned hate crime charges.[11]

This prompted a significant debate about whether the hate crime charges were actually warranted. An unsigned editorial in the *Baltimore Sun* argued that what had transpired in Princess Anne may have violated the law, but did not constitute a hate crime per se. "Equating an act of political vandalism with violence against a person because of his or her race, ethnicity, religion or other protected characteristic cheapens the very idea of a hate crime," wrote the editorial's author.[12]

In the end, the authorities agreed. Less than a week after the two women were arrested, the hate crime charges were dropped, though the others—including malicious burning and trespassing—remained.[13] Semantics matter, and the outcry over this particular event shines a particular light on just why that's the case.

*   *   *

As the scuffle over political signs in Newark showed, some regions have opted to outlaw political signage entirely in the lead-up to elections, whether local or national. But going that route encountered its own obstacles, ones far more all-encompassing than someone looking to take down a poster or replace a yard sign with one for their preferred candidate.

That changed in 2015, when the Supreme Court released its ruling in *Reed v. Town of Gilbert*. The ruling concerned an Arizona town—namely, Gilbert—which had enacted a complex system of guidelines related to signage within the municipality. That law was challenged by a local church, which ultimately led to the case being heard before the nation's highest court. The result was a unanimous decision against Gilbert's ordinance, with the majority opinion written by Clarence Thomas. It also led Elena Kagan to wrly observe, in her concurring opinion, that "[t]his Court may soon find itself a veritable Supreme Board of Sign Review."[14]

At SCOTUSblog, legal journalist Lyle Denniston explored some of the implications of the Court's decision.

> The Thomas opinion in the public sign case was based upon a brand-new theory that, whenever a law addresses different forms of public expression, and treats them differently, it is a form of regulation of the message in each mode, which amounts to discrimination in violation of the First Amendment. Moreover, the theory requires that such differing treatment be judged by "strict scrutiny"— the most demanding constitutional test.[15]

What that comes down to, then, is that political signage is treated as any other sort of expression or speech, making it nearly impossible to regulate. While some regulations do protect polling places from being bombarded with campaign signage, that's the exception rather than the rule. And so, the ubiquity of signage in the landscape around elections seems unlikely to go away any time soon. Looks like the sign wars will be with us for a while longer.

3 THE BUSINESS OF SIGNS

"Advertising agencies have tried openly to sell Presidents since 1952."[1] That's Joe McGinniss writing in his 1969 book *The Selling of the President*, which focuses on the primary and general election campaigns of Richard Nixon. It's a fascinating book for a host of reasons, including the way it reverberates through subsequent decades of American political history—in it, you'll see the first glimpse of future Fox News head Roger Ailes on the national stage.

In his book, McGinniss notes that the Nixon operation wasn't the first presidential campaign to bring in a high-profile advertising agency. McGinniss's book is noteworthy in part because of the access he received to the Republican side of things. Early on in the book, he talks about how he had initially approached the Hubert Humphrey campaign and requested access, only to have his request turned down.

Plenty of things had to happen for McGinniss's book to still be widely read fifty years after its publication. First and foremost is how the 1968 election turned out; in other words, McGinniss had access to what turned out to be the winning side. But much of it also dovetails with growing trends in media: McGinniss makes a number of references throughout his book to the writings of media theorist Marshall McLuhan—which have been prophetic for decades now. And there's the presence of Ailes in the narrative, tying the story of one particular campaign to a broader narrative about American conservatism and the methods by which the media covers politics.

Alternately, *The Selling of the President* is a kind of political science version of *The Hobbit* in its role as a precursor to later chronicles of the successful campaigns of George W. Bush and Donald Trump.

*   *   *

For many Western democracies, the story of voting is one of a gradual expansion in voting rights. In some instances, the right to vote was limited due to race, gender, or property—or, as was the case in the early days of the United States, a combination of all three. As suffrage expanded to include more and more of the population, reaching even larger groups of the voting public became more of a concern.

An 1856 illustration of New York City's Tammany Hall displays it festooned with banners that don't look all that different from the political signage of 150 years later. Both banners are approximately one story in height: One extols the James Buchanan/John Breckenridge ticket for President and Vice President, while the other promotes Fernando Wood's candidacy for mayor;[2] another illustration, this one from eight years later, displays a crowd of people holding along signs for George McClellan's run for the presidency.[3]

That doesn't mean that nineteenth-century examples of political signage are eminently recognizable as such. A broadsheet in support of George B. McClellan's unsuccessful presidential campaign in 1864, for instance, features an image of the candidate looking heroic, with the phrase "McClellan For President" immediately below. So far, so good. But immediately below that are lyrics for a song arguing that McClellan would make a better head of state than then-incumbent Abraham Lincoln.[4] And while songs have gone on to be an essential part of many a campaign—Lee Greenwood of "God Bless the USA" fame supported Donald Trump's campaign, for instance—you don't see many direct allusions to songs, original or repurposed, directly on signage these days.

Other forms of political signage suggest that the past was a more verbose time. A flyer for the Abraham Lincoln/ Hannibal Hamlin ticket in 1860 contains several paragraphs, including one comprised of a single sprawling sentence which alludes to "the complete overthrow and defeat of the corrupt and unscrupulous Sham-Democracy."[5] To be fair, the country was on the verge of a literal civil war at this time. Even so, it's a particularly harsh choice of phrase. One can only imagine what the 1860 version of Twitter would have made of it.

The refinement and professionalization of political campaign signage was a gradual process. Bruce Barton, one of the founders of the ad agency Batten, Burston, Durstine, and Osborn, had acted as an adviser to Republican candidates beginning in 1924.[6] Barton himself went beyond the role of adviser, spending two years in the House of Representatives. He's arguably best known for writing the book *The Man Nobody Knows*, which blended ruminations on the life of Jesus Christ with thoughts on how Christ's organization skills might be harnessed for the corporate world. A 2016 article by Yoni Applebaum in *The Atlantic* noted Barton's rhetorical and ideological similarity to another unorthodox Republican from New York: Donald Trump. These similarities included pledges to run the government in the style of a business and efforts to repeal laws simply for the sake of repealing laws.[7]

The advertising agency Young & Rubicam began working with Dwight Eisenhower's presidential campaign in 1952—generally hailed as a seismic event for political advertising in the United States. The connection between the two predated that moment, however: agency co-founder John Orr Young had led efforts, beginning in 1947, to coax the onetime war hero into running for office.[8] By the time his re-election campaign was in full force four years later, Eisenhower's birthday was celebrated via a special televised on CBS, known as Ike Day.[9] David Haven Blake, author of a book on Eisenhower's campaigns and the prevalence of celebrity politics, wrote in a 2016 essay that the Democratic response balanced condemnation with contradiction.

> Faced with the barrage of endorsements for their opponent, Democrats responded like punch-drunk boxers immobilized in the ring. The Stevenson campaign criticized the cult of personality created by the hype, mocking both the quest for celebrity backers and the glamorization of political candidates. But even as they objected, the Democrats were planning their own televised special in which the likes of Eleanor Roosevelt, Bette Davis, Orson Welles and Elvis Presley would denounce the influence of advertising on politics. The idea never got past the draft stage.[10]

For better or for worse, we're now living in the world created by that blend of Eisenhower and advertising agencies. But even as television spots (and, more recently, online advertisements) look shinier and newer than old-school political signage, the same styles and techniques used in bygone decades continue to endure. In his essay "Cybernation and Culture," Marshall McLuhan wrote about "[t]he story line as a method of organizing data."[11] Modern political campaigning is certainly a place where data and storytelling converge, inexorably connected.

* * *

Sometimes signs don't even need a name on them to be effective. Perhaps the most seismic example of this came in

1988, when the people of Chile took to the polls in a plebiscite to determine if Augusto Pinochet would continue to rule the nation unopposed. (At the time, he had been in power for fifteen years, after a coup overthrew the government of Salvador Allende.) The plebiscite features one of the most pared-down ballots ever: it displayed Pinochet's name with two lines below it, one for yes (SI) and one for no (NO).

This, in turn, led to both campaigns making extensive use of advertisement, including nightly blocks of 15 minutes in length leading up to the election. The logo of the "NO" campaign featured the word in front of a rainbow's arc—the rainbow, in turn, represented the coalition of opposition parties seeking to end Pinochet's time in office.

That sign wasn't the only method by which advocates of the "NO" position made their positions known. Future Pulitzer Prize winner Eugene Robinson set the stage in his *Washington Post* article about the plebiscite, with a dispatch from Lo Hermida, a neighborhood within the city of Santiago.

All campaign activity was prohibited on election day, and it was a crime even to wear a "yes" or "no" button. But Lo Hermida was clearly "no" country. Residents indicated their preferences as they walked toward the polls, wagging their forefingers back and forth—a trademark gesture of the "no" campaign.[12]

The effect, then, is of a political revolution waged through symbols, logos, and advertising. Decades after it took place, the plebiscite and the rival campaigns were the subject of a fictionalized narrative film in Chile which was nominated for an Academy Award. "This is our change to overthrow the dictatorship," an activist, José Tomás Urrutia, in Pablo Larraín's 2012 film *No* tells the protagonist, René Saavedra. *No* focuses on the way this ideological battle played out in the media. (Larraín reportedly shot a longer version that also focused on activists working to increase voter turnout,[13] but these scenes were cut for the final version.) It's the rarest of creatures: a film about semiotics that's also a compelling narrative.

Not every single-word campaign ends on a progressive victory. In 2016, residents of the United Kingdom voted on whether or not to stay in the European Union (EU). This in turn led to the landscape being populated by signs for the rival "VOTE LEAVE" and "VOTE REMAIN" campaigns. The latter's logo took the last two letters of "REMAIN" and added a color scheme reminiscent of the Union Jack—a neatly done bit of reinforcement of the campaign's notion that remaining in the EU could be a patriotic gesture.

In a close vote, the Leave campaign won the day, paving the way for several years of upheaval in British politics and (arguably) anticipating the election of Donald Trump in the United States several months later. But this in turn led to the debate that followed the vote, and perhaps explains the contentious debates that swallowed British politics in the aftermath of the Brexit vote: namely, how does one leave the EU on a national level?

The aftermath of the referendum on EU membership involved more than a few postmortems on each campaign.

Writing for *Ad Age*, Emma Hall and Alexandra Jardine contrasted what worked and what didn't work about each campaign. Among the experts in the field quoted is Jon McLeod, the chair of corporate, financial, and public affairs for the London branch of the public relations firm Weber Shandwick. He told Hall and Jardine that one of the issues with the campaign came down to the choice of a particular word.

"Remain is a very difficult word from a neuro-linguistic point of view—they should have gone with 'Stay,' which has much more warmth and positivity," he said.[14] Three years after the vote, Will Craig of the pro-Leave group Britain Stronger in Europe looked back on the campaigns—in part due to the release of *Brexit: The Uncivil War*, a drama that aired on Channel 4 in the UK and HBO in the United States. At *The Guardian*, he wrote that "[t]he programme does a decent job of demonstrating how Vote Leave used a superior slogan ("Take back control") and false claims (on money for the NHS, and Turkey joining the EU) to capture the public mood."[15]

That may be one of the most unsettling elements of the Brexit vote: the fact that numerous statements touted as facts by the Leave campaign turned out to be completely false, including a promise of increased spending for the National Health Service and the ease of negotiating a trade deal with the EU.[16] And that, too, is one of the more disorienting elements of political signage over the years: it doesn't need to be accurate to be effective. What happens when a winning campaign turns out to have been built around a lie?

4 THE PROS AND CONS OF BEING GENERIC

Let's talk about templates for a moment. Plenty of political signs use them: a swooping banner, a strong font, a name front and center. Numerous political signs fit into certain parameters—making them easy to replicate, primed to parody, and simpler than you might think to hack.

In 2004, the Republican ticket of George W. Bush and Dick Cheney was running for re-election. As political campaigns from all parties are prone to do, they decided to experiment with technology and, presumably, give their supporters something interesting to use on the internet. And so an online sign generator was born: Users could go to the Bush/Cheney campaign's website, type in a certain message, and create a PDF that could be printed out, laminated, and hung wherever that voter wanted. In theory, this was perfect. Someone could create the personalized sign of their dreams: MORRIS COUNTY VETERANS FOR BUSH, for example, or LABRADOODLE OWNERS FOR BUSH/CHENEY. These were, for all intents and purposes, formal campaign posters; the signs generated by the tool featured, according to one article, "a disclaimer stating that the poster was paid for by Bush-Cheney '04, Inc."[1]

That was the ideal. In practice, it went a little bit differently.

The tool was launched in December 2013; by early the following year, a number of people who weren't exactly fans of the Bush/Cheney ticket had discovered it—and, as frequently happens on the internet, they began using it toward absurd ends. A March 12, 2004 article from *WIRED* documented precisely what had happened: Ana Marie Cox, founding editor of the political website Wonkette, notified her readers of the tool and called for suggestions on signs that could be generated through it. The result was enough to make fans of surreal and irreverent humor laugh hysterically—and likely made some Bush/Cheney campaign staffers apoplectic.

> At Cox's request, close to 200 Wonkette readers sent in slogans which they had slipped through the system. Among them: "Run for your lives," "They sure smell like old people," and the Orwellian, "A boot stomping on a human face forever."[2]

Not long after that, the Bush team altered the tool so that users could only select from a list of preapproved statements, rather than the endlessly customizable, eminently gameable system that they'd previously established. This poorly thought out element of the digital strategy of an otherwise successful campaign does point to something larger: namely, the fact that political signage frequently hews to certain easily identifiable templates.

If you'd like to go online to purchase a yard sign for your own political campaign, you can easily find a template to do so, and the same design and color scheme can be used by candidates from rival parties, by potential officeholders from sheriff to senator, and for residents of nearly anywhere there's turf to put one's stake into.

This has a twofold effect. First, it means that anyone with even a passing knowledge of political signage can almost instantly recognize a political sign when they see it. In the United States, that generally means stars and flags; sometimes it might it also mean a donkey or an elephant, but the traditional party symbols seems to have declined in use in recent decades. Perhaps that's a result of political messaging; perhaps it's due to the fact that neither animal is exactly the most flattering creature to be compared with.

The second means, paradoxically speaking, that some of the most memorable political signs are those that don't adhere to this template. This isn't always true; history is littered with examples of political campaigns whose signs defied convention, and whose chosen candidates failed at the ballot box as a direct result of it. The same is true for most forms of advertising. The line between "groundbreaking" and "interesting failure" is a fine one. Some political signs may have worked wonderfully on paper, but failed miserably once actual voters encountered them.

The aforementioned sameness of many a political sign also directly relates to how politics are depicted in visual forms of media: for purposes of this book, I'm talking about movies, television, and comics. Watching a movie about a fictional sports team often inspires some cognitive dissonance, in that there's a sense of something being off about most fictional teams' uniforms and logos in various forms of media compared with the real thing. This happens far less frequently when it comes to depictions of political campaigns in visual media.

For example, that sense of dissonance doesn't come to mind when watching *Tanner '88*, Robert Altman and Gary Trudeau's fictional documentary about a presidential candidate. Nor does it come to mind in Warren Ellis and Darick Robertson's science-fiction comic *Transmetropolitan*, about a journalist navigating unethical politicians in a technologically advanced future. The image of Orson Welles's character at a campaign rally frequently associated with the film *Citizen Kane* is still easily identifiable as a scene set at a political rally, even though Welles's film was released almost eighty years ago.

It's one of the few places in modern society where the genericness of a given object work to its advantage. And it's one of the reasons that so many films and television shows have used the world of politics as their setting, including—but not limited to—*My Fellow Americans*; *Boss*; *Dave*; *The*

West Wing; *Veep*; *Yes, Minister*; *Yes, Prime Minister*; *Swing Vote*; *The Campaign*; *The Candidate*; *The Politician*; *The Trotsky*; *The Thick of It*; *The Wire*.

Perhaps the apotheosis of political signs on screen came from the mind of writer-director Dee Rees. In "Kill All Others," a short film produced as part of the Channel 4/ Amazon co-production *Philip K. Dick's Electric Dreams*, Rees opted to very loosely adapt Dick's story "The Hanging Stranger." "Kill All Others" focuses on Philbert, an everyman working in a factory at some unspecified point in the near future. Philbert becomes alarmed by the rise of a populist candidate with a penchant for slipping the phrase "kill all others" into her speeches and interviews. Even more alarming to Philbert, the people around him either don't seem to notice, or ask why, precisely, he's so in favor of these mysterious "others."

As Philbert's fear and confusion grow, he begins to see the title phrase on signs and billboards nearly everywhere he goes. In an article for the film site IndieWire, writer Chris O'Falt interviewed production designer Julie Berghoff. Berghoff described a contrast between the classical aesthetic of some of the architecture on display in these scenes and the horrific message of the signage, telling O'Falt that Philbert "passes all this very classic middle class architecture, along with the 'Kill All Others' digital signs popping up."[3]

The climax of Rees's short film involves a massive piece of political signage: a huge billboard reading "KILL ALL OTHERS" on which a person has seemingly been lynched.

It's a thoroughly harrowing sequence, one in which Philbert himself becomes entangled with the sign that so horrified him. Rees's film reads like a direct reaction to a rise of reactionary populism around the globe, and in its depiction of a character trying and failing to avoid signs and symbols of that movement, it achieved a haunting resonance. It also served as a reminder of the power of speculative fiction to transform the quotidian into something extraordinary—or, in this case, into something horrific. What happens when a political sign turns from the quotidian into the murderous? Rees's film offers one answer, and it's one with unsettling implications for the audience taking it in at home.

5 POLITICAL SIGNS IN THE PUBLIC EYE

There are moments in election campaigns that might make observers lament the dearth of civility in campaigning these days. And then there are moments that recall nothing so much as football hooliganism at its apex—or zenith, depending on your take on the matter. In the fall of 2018, Scott Wagner, the Republican candidate for governor of Pennsylvania, took to Facebook Live to express his displeasure with incumbent Tom Wolf.

Well, "express his displeasure" might be putting it mildly. In his remarks directed to Wolf, Wagner told him that "you better put a catcher's mask on your face because I'm gonna stomp all over your face with golf spikes because I'm gonna win this for the state of Pennsylvania."[1]

What led to Wagner's fury? Had Wolf publicly slapped him in the face with a glove and then challenged him to a duel? Had Wolf, perhaps, left a particularly rude comment on Wagner's AirBnB profile page? Had he urinated all over Wagner's favorite rug, then set the rug on fire, and then written slanderous comments besmirching the honor of Wagner and his entire family in ink made using the ashes of the urine-stained rug?

No, no, and no. What prompted Wagner to vent his rage—in a video that was subsequently deleted—was a billboard, located on Route 581 near the city of Harrisburg.[2] The ad critiqued Wagner's company, Penn Waste, for having sued nearly 7,000 Pennsylvania residents; it was paid for by Pennsylvania Spotlight, a politically left-of-center advocacy group.[3] And it led to what could have charitably been called a meltdown on Wagner's part: Nothing says "take this candidate seriously" like threatening violence against your opponent with that post-apocalyptic weapon known as golf spikes, after all.

What was terrible for Wagner's public image was also a fine reminder that billboards still have plenty of sticking power in the minds of voters and politicians alike.

*　*　*

Living in New York City in 1977 had its high points—the dawn of hip-hop, a thriving punk scene, and a great season for the Yankees among them. It also had some unpleasant elements, notably the presence of the Son of Sam serial killer and an infamous summer blackout. But New York in 1977 was also home to one of the most contentious uses of political signage in history. It took place during the 1977 Democratic primary for that fall's mayoral election, and it involved a political sign that may or may not have been created with the consent of one of the candidates.

Facing off in the primary were Ed Koch and Mario Cuomo. History doesn't get spoiler alerts, so I'll say from the outset that Koch won; Cuomo had to settle for three terms as governor of the state beginning in 1983. For most of his life in public office, Koch was rumored to be gay and closeted. This would later come up in enduring criticisms of Koch's administration for not taking enough steps to stop the spread of AIDS. It was this particular rumor that the signs addressed, in one of the crudest ways imaginable.

In 2015, Jonathan Mahler at *The New York Times* explored the long rivalry between Koch and Cuomo, one which had its beginnings in that summer's contentious primary.

> The friction was exacerbated by the appearance of posters in Mr. Cuomo's native borough of Queens telling people to "Vote for Cuomo, Not the Homo." Mr. Cuomo denied having anything to do with the posters, but Mr. Koch never forgave him for them.[4]

Questions persist as to whether or not this was officially sanctioned by Cuomo's campaign. A *Village Voice* article from 1982 noted otherwise, stating that "his gay rights record, which dates at least from his issuing of an antidiscrimination executive order on becoming secretary of state in 1974, has been unambiguous."[5]

Almost thirty years later, the posters continued to haunt some of the people involved—in this case, Mario's son Andrew Cuomo, who had worked on his father's campaign in 1977 and who, in 2006, was running his own campaign for New York State Attorney General. Patrick D. Healy reported on Cuomo's visit to the Stonewall Democratic Club of NYC, which had been founded in 1986 as "the first and only citywide LGBT Democratic organization in New York City."[6] At the event, Healy reported, one member of the audience raised the possibility that the younger Cuomo had been responsible for the anti-Koch posters. Cuomo's response was to call that accusation an "ugly, cheap, untrue rumor."[7]

Four years later, Cuomo continued to deal with the fallout from the posters. A 2010 *New York Times* article by Michael Barbaro pointed out that Cuomo faced doubts about his commitment to gay rights and marriage equality. Here, too, the specter of 1977 came up.

> Mr. Koch said he had accepted an apology from the younger Mr. Cuomo for the tone of that race. But asked recently in an interview if he believed that Andrew Cuomo had nothing to do with the homophobic posters, Mr. Koch said: "I honestly don't know. I'd like to believe it. But I don't know."[8]

Voters have a long memory, and the anti-Koch posters are the kinds of things people who saw them aren't likely to forget. The same posters that someone—whether sanctioned by Cuomo's campaign or not—unveiled in an attempt to defeat Ed Koch in the primary instead resulted in Mario Cuomo's defeat in the primary election. The fact that decades later, the legacy of those posters continued to haunt Andrew Cuomo—both in his political relationships and in speculation about his stances on political issues—shows the kind of power political signage can wield, and how it can backfire.

Mario Cuomo was known for his fondness for the phrase "You campaign in poetry; you govern in prose."[9] But that's the tricky thing about political signs: they're neither poetry nor prose, and in the space between the two some unexpected dissonances can crop up—dissonances with consequences of their own.

6 SIGNS AS SHORTHAND, SIGNS AS REMAKES

The right billboard in the right place can serve as a bold visual cue or a meaningful timestamp. Novelist Stephen King has worked politics into plenty of his novels—1979's *The Dead Zone*, in which a populist presidential candidate turns out to be a sociopath, is especially prescient in exactly the way a horror novel should be. And even when he isn't addressing politics directly, King has a penchant for using political signage as shorthand for characterization, whether for an individual or to give a sense of the pulse of a specific region.

Jake Epping, the protagonist of King's novel *11/22/63*, ventures back in time to prevent the assassination of John F. Kennedy. The novel abounds with the placement of a contemporary man in the late 1950s and early 1960s—including a reminder that political polarization in the United States didn't begin in the early 2000s. As Epping heads into

Dallas, he takes in the signage around him and discovers himself in a part of the country where tempers run high and billboards seem to be shouting out their messages:

> There were billboards advocating the impeachment of Supreme Court Chief Justice Earl Warren; billboards showing a snarling Nikita Khruschev (NYET, COMRADE KHRUSHCHEV, the billboard copy read, WE WILL BURY *YOU!*); there was one on West Commerce Street that read THE AMERICAN COMMUNIST PARTY FAVORS INTEGRATION. **THINK ABOUT IT!** That one had been paid for by something called the Tea Party Society.[1]

The Tea Party Society, cultural critic Frank Rich noted, was King's own invention[2]—a way to tie the furious right-wing politics of the early 1960s to the furious right-wing politics of the Obama era. The rest of the billboards were entirely real. And even when presented in more toned-down terms, King can still invoke political ephemera as shorthand for political ideology—and perhaps a general philosophy of life. Consider these two quotes from his novel *The Outsider*, set in the aftermath of the 2016 election, both describing objects found on cars.

> She was a middle-aged nurse wearing a tunic covered with dancing teddy bears. Her car was an old Honda Civic with rust on the sides, a cracked taillight that had been mended

with duct tape, and a fading I'M WITH HILLARY sticker on the bumper.[3]

And here, a political bumper sticker contrasts with a decidedly nonideological one.

> A minivan pulled in ahead of Holly's Prius. On one side of the bumper was a sticker reading MOM'S TAXI. The one on the other side read I BELIEVE IN THE 2ND AMENDMENT, **AND I VOTE**.[4]

Many of King's novels focus on characters who appear to be one thing and turn out to be something else entirely—*The Outsider* in particular is full of those kinds of reversals. On one hand, he's using political bumper stickers as a shorthand for characterization; on the other, he's doing so in a larger narrative that warns against taking such judgments for granted.

But most people don't have the luxury of that sort of expansive empathy in their everyday lives. See the right bumper sticker—an "Abortion Stops a Beating Heart," say, or a faded Obama/Biden 2008 sticker—and you're liable to make certain assumptions about the owner of that vehicle. And, to an extent, the owner of that vehicle has also chosen to identify herself as such: an Obama voter, an anti-abortion voter, a concerned environmentalist, a frustrated libertarian. Why talk when you can just glower at the assumed persona of the driver in front of you, waiting for the light to change?

* * *

One of the most seismic political advertisements in recent memory was the product of advertising agency Saatchi & Saatchi in 1978. A 2007 article in *The Independent* called it "a political poster that is probably the most effective ever produced."[5] The first thing you see is a stark white background, on which a sprawling line of people waits at the door of an unemployment office. (The image used in the ad was not a documentary; playing the role of frustrated job seekers were members of Hendon Young Conservatives.[6]) Atop the line, in stark black text, was the slogan: LABOUR ISN'T WORKING. In much smaller type near the bottom, you could see a line indicating the origin of the ad: "Britain's Better Off With The Conservatives."

The advertisement first appeared in 1978, when the United Kingdom's Prime Minister seemed to be on the verge of calling for a new general election. When that election was held the following year, Conservatives brought it back out—and used it as the centerpiece of a victory that would leave Margaret Thatcher as Prime Minister for over a decade. Ironically, Thatcher herself was skeptical of the ad at first, unsure why her party should make use of something with the opposition party's name in such a prominent position.

In an article written for the British media publication *Campaign* in 2018, Martyn Walsh—an art director at Saatchi & Saatchi who worked on the "Labour Isn't Working" campaign—provided an inside look at the development of this ad. The effectiveness of the ad was one thing—but it also sparked a controversy which led to even more publicity for the ad campaign. All publicity isn't necessarily good publicity, but in this case, it was. As Walsh described it:

> Immediately every newspaper put it on their front page, every TV station had it on the news, and the more Labour kept talking about it, the more coverage it received. By the end of the first week, both the poster and the name Saatchi & Saatchi were known in every household in Britain.[7]

Martyn closes his reminiscence with an allusion to a very different political moment. After the campaign had been deemed a success, the agency's co-founder Charles Saatchi asked Martyn what he wanted as a kind of bonus for his work. Martyn requested "a print that was rarely seen by anyone, was totally unloved and in the corner it had a crack in the glass."[8] That artwork? Richard Hamilton's *Kent State*, which depicted a wounded anti-war protestor at Kent State in 1970.[9] Sometimes politics can be strange; that one of the minds behind a campaign that propelled Margaret Thatcher into high office would choose as his reward a work of art that showed a man injured for opposing Richard Nixon's foreign policy is a particularly notable example of this.

The success of this campaign led to a long and successful partnership between Saatchi & Saatchi and the Conservative Party, one that lasted until 2007, when the agency submitted a successful proposal for the campaign of Labour Prime Minister Gordon Brown—though by that time, the agency's founders had left; their subsequent agency, M&C Saatchi, continued to work for the Conservative Party. Charles's brother Maurice spent several years as the chair of said party, from 2003 to 2005.

But to look at "Labour Isn't Working" as a kind of breakout political hit doesn't quite do justice to its impact—or the bleaker side of its influence. Thirty-eight years after one seismic right-wing political party used the imagery of an endless line in their signage, another British party opted for an ad campaign that played like a bizarre and unsettling echo of it.

In 2016, Nigel Farage of the far-right UK Independence Party unveiled a new large-scale print advertisement in advance of the forthcoming Brexit vote. Here, the endless line was depicted as one of immigrants; atop the image were the words "BREAKING POINT."[10] The ad campaign resulted in a significant blowback for Farage: the poster was accused of violating a law designed to prevent hatred on the basis of race, and one sharp-eyed observer noted that the UKIP's preferred design evoked nothing so much as Nazi propaganda.[11]

Farage's preferred poster is, in fact, a thoroughly dehumanizing piece of work, where racist scare tactics run rampant. While it differs from the Tories' ad campaign in one significant respect—that is, the Tories attempt to create a sense of empathy for the people depicted on the poster, while the UKIP want anything but that—it looks like nothing so much as an ill-advised remake, made on a shoestring and hastening something disastrous.

*   *   *

The Brexit campaign and its aftermath have seen distinctive political posters emerge from multiple sides of the political divide. Thankfully, Farage's hard-right faction isn't the only one creating distinctive work; there's also the satirical work of the group Led By Donkeys, which makes pointed use of billboards both physical and projected.

What has that entailed? A mug shot-style illustration of a chastened Boris Johnson holding up a sign reading "I LIED TO THE QUEEN" after Johnson's attempt to suspend Parliament was deemed unconstitutional by the country's Supreme Court in late 2019, for one.[12] Another campaign featured billboards with massive quotes from members of the Nigel Farage–led Brexit Party, in which party leaders and candidates for office advocated for politically unpopular positions such as dismantling the country's healthcare system and publicly shaming breastfeeding.[13]

In the fall of 2019, Led By Donkeys held a competition to reinvent the Johnson government's "Get Ready for Brexit" ad campaign. Among the judges was Armando Iannucci, known for his work on satirical films and television shows like *The Thick of It*, *Veep*, and *The Death of Stalin*.[14] The winning billboards included one featuring Donald Trump devouring the National Health Service, and another in which Johnson's face was given makeup resembling Pennywise, the demonic clown at the center of Stephen King's horror novel *It*.[15]

Led By Donkeys frequently make use of another terse and ephemeral form of communication with their billboard work: they frequently display old Tweets from pro-Brexit politicians to call them out for hypocritical behavior. One cites Boris Johnson, circa 2017, arguing that a "no deal" Brexit was impossible;[16] another called him out for a wavering position on the importance of parliamentary democracy.[17] And their work hasn't been limited to British politicians: when Donald Trump visited London in June of 2019, Led By Donkeys projected images referencing his political rivals Barack Obama and John McCain on buildings throughout the city.[18]

The work of Led By Donkeys occupies a space between many traditions: It borrows some of the tools of political signage yet stands apart from it, and it neatly conflates the physical and the digital. The result is a fascinating and effective blend of new and old, an innovative way to make a point, sometimes by repurposing the words of their political rivals. And given the groundswell of attention and support the group has received, their message—equal parts conceptual and direct—has hit home for many.

7 ON PROTEST SIGNS

I can't remember the first time I took part in a political demonstration. That isn't an attempt to prove my *bona fides* as far as political actions are concerned; to be honest, I've taken part in far fewer protests and demonstrations than my ideals would like. I don't remember my first protest or demonstration or rally—feel free to choose your preferred term—because I simply wasn't old enough to do so.

When I was a small child, my mother took me to a demonstration in favor of the Equal Rights Amendment. I don't remember exactly where it took place, though I suspect it was in Asbury Park by virtue of Asbury Park being one of the few local towns with public spaces sizable enough to host a rally. It might be more appropriate to say that, to the extent that any memory of it exists, it's become blurred together in my mind's eye with other outings with my mother: the time in the early 1980s when her car broke down and needed to be towed, or our walk down the shore to watch my dad compete in a marathon one misty autumn day.

I still have a souvenir from the rally, though: a green button, about two inches in diameter, with the phrase "ERA

YES" emblazoned on it in white, angular letters. The button was an omnipresent element of my childhood, something to sit on the shelves of my bedroom beside Matchbox cars, pictures of dinosaurs, and snow globes.

For the first few years I had it, I don't even think I knew what it meant. As far as I knew, it was simply expressing a positive opinion toward an era. Which era? Clearly that wasn't all that important.

By the time I was old enough to start caring about politics—formative influences included punk rock, a penchant for being contrary, and writer Ann Nocenti's run on *Daredevil*—it still took me too long to look back at that green button and parse out what that actually meant. Sometimes the signs and symbols around you your whole life become so ubiquitous they lose all meaning. See also: my status as a lapsed Episcopalian.

So I started learning things about what the Equal Rights Amendment had been about. We were a couple of years into the 1990s at this point; my source of this information was, by and large, my mom. But in learning about what the ERA stood for—and the fact that it had been blocked for decades by elements of movement conservatism—helped me clarify my own politics. Equality based around gender struck me then as a decidedly laudable and noncontroversial goal; the fact that there were some in the country who felt that it was too far beyond the pale ended up giving me a good sense of where I stood politically. Funny how that works out.

That preschool-aged version of me may have had a penchant for devouring Play-Doh and was apparently somewhat of a schoolyard bully for the under-5 set, but his politics turned out to have been pretty solid.

*   *   *

In the fall of 2000, I was 24 years old. I hadn't traveled much when I was in college—one family vacation was pretty much the extent of it. And I didn't travel much between college and my hometown, either: an hour-long bus ride was all it took to get me from one to the other, traffic permitting. And so the week after Thanksgiving, I boarded a plane and flew across the country to visit Seattle and Portland for the first time.

The bulk of my trip was spent in Seattle; the record label my friend Scott and I were running at the time was working with a few musicians based out there, which was also how I happened to have a couch to crash on for the Seattle leg of the trip. I hadn't planned on taking in one of the largest protests I've ever seen or getting my first look up close at police decked out in riot gear, waiting for something to go wrong.

Turns out that my trip to Seattle coincided with the one-year anniversary of the G-7 protests that had shaken the city a year before. The anniversary protests, which took place near Pike Place Market, were—so far as I can tell—one part commemoration of the earlier protest and one part reminder that the issues that had been raised in those protests had still not been resolved.

This was a particularly strange time for American politics. At that point, the recount of ballots in Florida was still underway; George W. Bush and Al Gore each awaited word of which of them would be found victorious. It was, for all intents and purposes, Schrödinger's Presidential Election. Throw in the anti-globalization critiques—still largely a left-of-center phenomenon (see also: Ralph Nader's Green Party run that year)—and you can see (in retrospect) both the buckling of one strain of left-wing politics and the early crystallization of the populism that would become a much larger factor in American politics by the time of the 2016 election.

The protests abounded with signs. So many signs, and so many costumes. Signs decrying the World Bank's policies against developing countries, signs denouncing corporate greed, signs lamenting environmental catastrophes. I have a very distinct memory of a cluster of people in turtle costumes; it's strange what sticks with you after all these years.

In one photograph, two signs in close proximity illustrate the range of aesthetics that could be seen. One protestor holds aloft a mass-printed blue sign with white and green text. On it reads a slogan using repetition that would make Hemingway proud: "WTO: it doesn't work for working families: it doesn't work." A few feet away, another protestor holds another sign aloft, this one hand-painted. It featured the letters "WTO" in black inside of a red circle with a slash through it. Other signs offered broader criticisms of capitalism and support of protest movements in general. "Down With The Market;

Up With People" was emblazoned on one long banner. An even longer one—wider than most protestors were tall—was labeled "Honoring Histories of Resistance," and featured images of past protests at Alcatraz and Attica.

Reader, I was a dilettante and a tourist. I walked around the protestors and took plenty of photos and did my best to take in the spectacle. I felt very much as though I was documenting something rather than being an active participant. At the time, that felt fine to me. I ran a zine; I did some freelance writing. I was part of the media. This is what the media did, right?

I broke away from the protests for a little bit and wandered around the Seattle waterfront. I got back to the protests as the sun was setting. My photos from this time are blurrier: I wasn't using my flash, and the demonstrators were in a constant state of motion and so was I. And then I turned my head and saw the police.

Now, the Seattle Police Department had been a presence throughout the day. But these were the cops in riot gear: helmets with visors and shields and batons. There was a line of them. I realized very quickly that, should anything happen, they were on one side and I was on the other. That, more than any one particular sign, helped some things fall into place for me politically that evening in Seattle.

Even so, I still took a photograph of the police lined up. I still have it.

*　　*　　*

Signs aiming to protect the environment and critique globalization weren't the only forms of protest signs on display at the anniversary protest in Seattle. Arguably the largest sign there was hoisted by a solitary figure. It was hand-illustrated and starkly lettered, and it argued that anyone who had not accepted Jesus Christ as their savior was bound for hell. I've seen signs like it on the sidewalks of many cities, but the one that afternoon in Seattle was immediately eye-catching: Between eight and ten feet high and carried over its bearer's head, on a multicolored backdrop, it bade protestors to pray for forgiveness. "Perhaps You Will Be SAVED From Hell," it read, along with allusions to a pair of Bible verses.

The evangelical counter-protesting that I saw there—and which I still see from time to time around New York, including one guy making a spectacle of himself near the New York Public Library on 42nd Street—also bears mentioning when discussing protest signs.

While protest signs are generally associated, historically speaking, with liberal or progressive movements, this serves as a reminder that that's not always the case. Protest signs advocating increased suffrage, seeking an end to discrimination, or calling for the end of a war (or of war in general) are certainly prominent in the historical record and quickly come to mind when the phrase "protest signs" is uttered. But no one, least of all the members of this movement, would consider those who banded together during Barack Obama's presidency under the banner of the Tea Party movement as liberal or progressive. And the

Tea Party are practically left-wing when compared with the Westboro Baptist Church, whose virulently antigay beliefs have led them to picket military funerals, among other grotesque displays of intolerance.

Protesting is a form of speech, and as such it is something that can represent a panoply of viewpoints. No one, whether progressive or reactionary, has full ownership over the concept of protest. And given that many protests and rallies these days can involve counterprotests—in some cases more populous than the original event—it's not hard to see this dichotomy in action. Though if you're there as an observer, you may decide before long that it makes more sense to choose a side.

8 THE MAKING OF A PROTEST SIGN

What frequently sets protest signs apart from other forms of political signage is their DIY spirit. There are, clearly, some exceptions, but by and large what you see on protest signs is a handmade quality. It's as though a protestor tapped into skills they last used in a middle-school art class—and I won't lie, it's pretty appealing.

Some protest signs utilize the traditional setup: a large piece of paper held aloft by a piece of wood or some other rigid object. Others opt for an even simpler structure: a large piece of cardboard held aloft by hand. Pizza boxes have proven popular in recent years, and why not? They are, after all, sturdy enough that they won't begin to topple over if not held properly. That, too, speaks to the ease of use of making a protest sign: you can create an elaborate collage, piecing together old photographs with a carefully plotted-out message and an intricate diagram. Or you can just write a quick message expressing your righteous anger on the back of a cardboard box and hold it aloft for as long as your arms will allow. It's the garage band of political signage.

In the fall of 2019, a new museum opened in New York City called Poster House. Their inaugural exhibit focused on many of the protest signs associated with the 2017 Women's March. Collections Manager Melissa Walker noted that some of the signs, and one in particular, spoke to the interconnectedness that certain protest signs possess. "A few images do transcend borders—the raised fist, for example, is almost universally accepted as an image of protest," she told me. "Rhymes and profanity also seem to be the accepted language of protest."

As Walker catalogued the museum's massive array of posters, she began to notice certain motifs within American protest signs. "After staring at the language and imagery of American protest for about two months, a pattern emerged," she told me. "Rosie the Riveter, the raised fist, Internet memes, and one poster in particular that became a guide to explore past protests."

That sign was one that demonstrated the intersectionality of protest movements. "One major component of the exhibition is a timeline that uses one of the more popular signs at the 2017 Women's March as category headers to list protests from American history," she said. "It reads, 'Black Lives Matter, Women's Rights are Human Rights, Science is Real, No Human is Illegal, Love is Love.'"

* * *

In the right hands, clothing can even serve as a kind of political protest. The most harrowing example of this may be the leather jacket worn by the artist and activist David Wojnarowicz in 1988. Over a pink triangle, the words sewn there spelled out a powerful and searing message: "IF I DIE OF AIDS - FORGET BURIAL - JUST DROP MY BODY ON THE STEPS OF THE F.D.A."[1]

As essayist and critic Olivia Laing pointed out in 2016, an image of Wojnarowicz wearing the jacket in question has continued to circulate in the years since it was taken, and since Wojnarowicz's own death in 1992. Laing points out that, after the death of Nancy Reagan, the image of Wojnarowicz making a powerful statement against the Reagan administration's handling of AIDS served as a necessary correction to those seeking to rewrite history to make Reagan's record on AIDS look better than it actually was.[2]

Another form of clothing as protest came in early 2017, when the Women's March targeted Donald Trump's inauguration with pushback over his sexism and numerous accusations of sexual assault. While protest signs abounded at the March, so too did the pink "pussyhats" worn by many marchers. Jayna Zweiman and Krista Suh were responsible for the initial design, which rapidly spread across the country. In a 2017 interview with *The Forward*, Zweiman—who was unable to travel to the March due to the aftereffects of an injury—looked to the design of the hats as a way to be present in the protests without being there.[3]

And, as writer Amy Oringel phrased it, the hats continued to act as a symbol of protest long after the March itself had come to an end.

The hat has appeared on the covers of The New York Times Magazine, Time Magazine and the New Yorker and also found its way onto the heads of Amy Schumer, Cate Blanchett, Missoni models at Milan Fashion Week and the "Make Way for Ducklings" statues on the Boston Common.[4]

There aren't many hats that can serve as ideological shorthand for a protest movement. These act as a notable exception to the rule.

*   *   *

Some of the power of protest signs can emerge from their collective power. One person standing in isolation holding a sign aloft can be evocative, but a sea of people, all with protest signs, can be overwhelmingly powerful in a decisive way. Consider one of the most haunting images of the Civil Rights Movement: striking sanitation workers in Memphis, each one carrying or wearing a sign reading "I <u>AM</u> A MAN."

A *Washington Post* article commemorating the strike's fiftieth anniversary offered the historical roots of why the signs resonate so deeply—then and now.

> "We felt we would have to let the city know that because we were sanitation workers, we were human beings. The signs we were carrying said 'I Am a Man,'" James Douglas, a sanitation worker, recalled in an American

Federation of State, County and Municipal Employees documentary. "And we were going to demand to have the same dignity and the same courtesy any other citizen of Memphis has."[5]

That doesn't mean that one person standing in isolation can't make a difference. During the presidency of George W. Bush, one woman earned both media attention and a kind of moral power for keeping a vigil outside the then-president's ranch in Crawford, Texas. The woman's name was Cindy Sheehan, and her son Casey had served in the United States military, dying in the war in Iraq in 2005.[6] Her stay lasted for four weeks, ending when Bush left Crawford to return to the White House due to Hurricane Katrina.[7]

The idea of a vigil for peace also has philosophical roots: when I was growing up, some of the first protests I can remember seeing were at the Quaker Meeting House across the street from the church where I would attend services with my mother. This being the early- to mid-1980s, most of the signs pertained more to nuclear disarmament than anything else, but it was still a powerful evocation of the impulse to seek political change through peaceful methods.

Look closely at almost any global conflict and you'll likely find images of Quakers espousing nonviolence as a response to it. A photograph taken in front of the White House during the Vietnam War features a group of people sitting on the sidewalk. One woman stands, supporting a sign that reads "QUAKER MEETING FOR WORSHIP FOR PEACE IN

VIETNAM."[8] It's an elegant reminder of the ways that protest, conviction, and faith can converge.

But the vigil as political protest can also lead to bleaker places. The technique of die-ins, in which a large number of people sprawl on the ground in a public place in order to evoke past or future deaths, has expanded its reach over the last few decades. In 2014, journalist Marina Koren noted its popularity related to some of the issues Black Lives Matter was bringing to the foreground and explored its history. Her findings suggested that it began with environmental activists working in the 1960s and 1970s, and acted as a dramatic way to demonstrate the dangers of pollution—and that they may have evolved out of the sit-ins popular among civil rights activists.[9]

The activism that coalesced around AIDS in the 1980s and 1990s also included die-ins. In a 2014 interview with writer, filmmaker, and historian Sarah Schulman—whose work includes an oral history of ACT UP and a documentary on the organization—she discussed the ways allusions to mortality factored in to the organization's work. "Many of the actions used symbolic representations of death," Schulman said. "So there'd be 'die-ins.' Or there'd be people lying on the ground holding up headstones, this type of thing."[10] Die-ins have also emerged as a technique of the gun control movement, with students in numerous cities in 2018 taking part in protests addressing gun control and mass shootings.[11]

There's an even bleaker aspect to these manifestations of the body as protest sign: the extreme gesture of self-immolation as a form of protest. It's a rare act, and surviving it is even more rare. And yet it continues: a *New York Times* article from 2013 noted that there were "nearly 100 Tibetans who have burned themselves to death in protest over Chinese rule."[12]

Decades earlier, a number of Buddhist monks had self-immolated as a way of protesting governmental policies in Vietnam. A 1966 article from *Time* looked back on protests that had taken place three years earlier, "when eight Buddhists burned themselves to death protesting President Ngo Dinh Diem's anti-Buddhist repressions."[13]

Self-immolation as a form of political protest has taken place around the world in recent years, and it is a particularly haunting way to make a message felt. What happens when one's own body is the sign with which one protests? And what happens when that protest involves destroying oneself?

9 SPORTS & SIGNS & SPONSORS

Fourth-division American soccer teams are generally not written about in the pages of *The New York Times*. To be fair, most fourth-division soccer teams in any location around the world wouldn't find themselves written up there—and yet, in the summer of 2012, a team that played at the Metropolitan Oval in New York City found themselves getting coverage from media outlets that far larger teams might long to receive a mention in.

Unfortunately, it wasn't for anything having to do with the way they were actually playing.

The team's name was FC New York, and the headlines came from the peculiar nature of their jersey sponsorship. (They should not be confused with New York City FC, who now play in Major League Soccer, but didn't exist at that point in soccer history.) While many soccer teams have the logos of well-known companies adorning the center of their jerseys—for US-based teams, Target, Herbalife, and Alaska Airlines all come to mind—FC New York took a somewhat different approach, which involved a stentorian former governor of Massachusetts then running for the highest office in the land.

On June 30, 2012, *The New York Times* featured a story about the team's new jersey sponsor: the Mitt Romney presidential campaign. The team's jerseys, going forward, were to feature the campaign's logo and the slogan "Believe in America." In this case, the Romney campaign wasn't exploring out-of-the-box advertising options. Instead, the funds came from a donor who preferred to remain anonymous.[1] "I love fútbol, I love America, I am a proud Latino-American who believes Mitt Romney needs to be our next president," the donor stated in a press release.[2]

Beside the article ran a photo of two players wearing the new jerseys. They looked—well, they looked like soccer jerseys. If you watch enough soccer, you can see virtually any kind of logo emblazoned on a team's kit, helping to promote everything from online betting services to Azerbaijani tourism. It turns out that there's a very good reason why political campaigns aren't seen more frequently in soccer.

Three days after the *Times* article about the Romney logos, *The Washington Times* broke a new development in the story: the sponsorship had been nixed.[3] FIFA, soccer's governing body, prohibits jersey sponsorships with political affiliations—and that was that. At least that was it for this particular team, which folded not long afterwards.

* * *

Most professional sports leagues—or, as in the case of FIFA, worldwide governing bodies for sports—enforce bans on political advertising. Nonetheless, there have been a few notable exceptions over the years, and a few unofficial political displays as well. That can speak to broader trends in the sports and leagues in question: Within the United States, one could convincingly argue that the NFL and NASCAR are more conservative, generally speaking, than the NBA and Major League Soccer. Is that a given for fans and participants in those leagues? Not at all, but the ways in which the NBA and NFL responded to the Black Lives Matter movement offers a telling study in contrasts.

One of the bolder displays of political advertising took place in the world of NASCAR. In February 2012, the conservative organization American Majority announced that it would sponsor driver Jason Bowles. At Politico, reporter Dave Levinthal covered the sponsorship and clarified that American Majority's status as a nonprofit restricted the ways it could advocate for certain policies via its sponsorship.

> The campaign, which will cost in the "seven-figure range," will not overtly advocate for a specific candidate or party—as a nonprofit educational organization, it can't— instead urging race fans to vote against big government, increased taxes and expanded national debt, American Majority President Ned Ryun said.[4]

American Majority, for those keeping track at home, is a nonprofit organization that trains conservative activists, and has done so since 2008. As of the writing of this chapter, their Twitter page boasted that they had trained over 39,000 people across the country. A statement on their website notes that their approach focuses on local races: "We believe meaningful, lasting political change starts not in Washington, but at state and local levels, where most actual government decisions and spending occurs."[5] Given the popularity of NASCAR—especially in 2012—it's not hard to see why this would appeal to American Majority.

But they're far from the only organization to explore a foray into the world of racing. Levinthal's article noted that this particular conservative group wasn't the only organization that's explored a racing sponsorship. "TeaParty. net last year sponsored [a] team in the NASCAR truck series," he wrote. "And in 2008, then-Sen. Barack Obama considered sponsoring a Sprint Cup race car, ultimately deciding against it."[6]

* * *

As mentioned earlier, FIFA regulations prevent politically oriented jersey sponsorships. But what about a jersey with a design that has inherently political connotations? Madureira Esporte Clube is a soccer team that plays in Brazil's third division. Their stadium is located in Estádio Conselheiro Galvão, in Rio de Janeiro's Madureira neighborhood.

Their roots date back to 1914, but it was in 1963 that one of the defining moments in their history occurred. That was when the team traveled to Cuba, then in its post-revolutionary heyday, as part of a promotional tour to cover many of their expenses. The team played a total of five games while on the island, winning all of them. In attendance for the fifth and final one was Che Guevara, at the time the nation's Minister of Industry, who met with several of the players and posed for photographs.[7]

Fifty years later, the team sought to commemorate that fateful meeting in some way. What emerged from this was a jersey with a familiar image of Guevara's face located on the right side, sprawling from the stomach to the back.[8] The goalkeeper kit takes things a step further, using a design inspired by the Cuban flag. On the back of the jersey, just below the collar, a quote from Guevara is inscribed: "Hasta la Victoria Siempre," which translates into "Until Victory Always."[9] A BBC report on the team's new kit noted that this was the first time Guevara's image had been used on a soccer jersey.[10]

The BBC's report on the jerseys also tapped into one of the perpetual ironies that surrounds Guevara: He's a Communist icon whose image has made a lot of money for capitalists over the years. The article noted that the jerseys had initially been used by the club's team in a seven-a-side league, but because of the attention they had drawn the club was considering expanding their use. "[T]he impact with football fans and Che Guevara supporters around the globe has been so positive that the club has been considering getting their main squad, which plays in the Brazilian third division, to wear the uniforms, too," wrote Lorena Arroyo of BBC Mundo.[11]

* * *

Political statements or messages on jerseys are largely prohibited by the bylaws of assorted sports leagues, teams, and governing bodies. But jerseys aren't the only things that athletes wear at arenas or stadiums, and plenty of athletes have turned their workout attire into signage bearing a particular political message. In the last decade, this practice in the NBA has attracted numerous headlines, which has also helped the league's reputation as the most progressively inclined men's league in the United States. Does that have its limits? It does—but the NBA stacks up well when, say, compared with the NFL's handling of players silently protesting during the playing of the national anthem.

One contributing factor is certainly the way that some of the NBA's most prominent players have taken the lead on these initiatives. In 2014, the death of Staten Island resident Eric Garner after a police officer used an unsanctioned chokehold on him sparked protests across the nation. Clothing emblazoned with the phrase "I can't breathe"— Garner's last words—was one of the signatures of the protest movement, a clarion call for justice following a man's horrific death.

Among those who donned garments with "I can't breathe" written on them were some of basketball's biggest names. When the Cleveland Cavaliers journeyed to Brooklyn to play the Nets in early December of 2014, Cavaliers players LeBron James and Kyrie Irving both sported shirts bearing the phrase as they warmed up before the game.[12] It wasn't the only instance of James taking a forceful political stance; following the election of Donald Trump two years later, James emerged as one of his highest-profile critics.[13]

In 2018, Sacramento police shot and killed Stephon Clark, an unarmed black man. The following year, the city agreed to pay his sons $2.4 million to settle the wrongful death lawsuit they had filed.[14] In the week following Clark's death, the NBA's Sacramento Kings were scheduled to host the Boston Celtics. On Sunday, March 25, players from both teams took to the court for warmups featuring shirts with Clark's name written on the back. Players also participated in a recorded statement that was shown before the game.[15]

> In the public service spot played on Sunday, Kings point guard De'Aaron Fox began, "These tragedies have to stop." He was followed by expressions of defiance from Kings guard Garrett Temple and Celtics forward Al Horford, who declared, respectively, "We will not stick to sports," and "We will not shut up and dribble."[16]

Elsewhere in the world of basketball, players in the WNBA has also been at the forefront of on-the-court political signage—even more so than their colleagues in the men's league. In the summer of 2016, a number of players from the Minnesota Lynx took to the court with the names of Alton Sterling and Minnesota resident Philandro Castile—both of whom had also been shot and killed by police—along with three politically charged phrases: "Black Lives Matter," "Change Starts With Us," and "Justice and Accountability."[17]

The protests spread from team to team, which initially drew some pushback from the league. Several teams and players were fined for wearing shirts other than regulation attire, which in turn led to a backlash against the league's management. Eventually, the WNBA's president, Lisa Borders, opted to rescind the fines and tweeted a statement in support of the players—or at least, in support of their right to express their political beliefs.[18]

Writing for Slate, Christina Cauterucci explained the significance of this. "Rarely have so many players and teams in a league stood together across racial lines on a matter of social import," she wrote. "Several NBA players, including the entire LA Lakers team, wore "I Can't Breathe" shirts in memory of Eric Garner in 2014, but it never spread to half the league, as the WNBA's stand for racial justice has."[19]

"We will not shut up and dribble," indeed. Players in both the NBA and WNBA have continued to take bold steps in support of their ideals—and in terms of racial justice, it's served as an inspiration for many across the nation.

10 SIGNS IN THE SEATS

Whether worn by players to express their beliefs or conveyed via a sponsorship agreement at the behest of a wealthy donor, there's a long history of political signage on athletes' uniforms or other gear. But when it comes to the other side of the equation—fans and supporters gathered together in a stadium to take in a game they love—political signage can also play a major role.

To take in a game of soccer in most locations is to experience a different kind of sporting event: singing for long durations of the match, supporters groups waving flags and pounding drums, and the unveiling of *tifo* before the game kicks off. For the uninitiated, *tifo* is an Italian word that refers to organized displays from supporters groups, some of which can be incredibly intricate, artistically complex, and politically charged.

The relationship between soccer and politics is a complex one: Eduardo Galeano's acclaimed book *Soccer in Sun and Shadow* explores the historical currents that unite the two. Elsewhere, particularly in Europe, certain cross-town rivalries have an added ideological wrinkle. The political dimensions of the relationships among three teams based in Madrid—Real Madrid, Atletico Madrid, and Rayo Vallecano—take on a particularly complex wrinkle when considered from a distance. As journalist Richard Ballout put it in a 2015 article for the soccer journal *FourFourTwo*, "[t]he accepted binary narrative of Real Madrid being the 'rich fascist elite' while Atleti are the 'good honest poor' is as outdated as it is simplistic."[1] That's not to say that there isn't a political dimension to their rivalry—only that it's more complicated than it seems.

Sometimes the politics of soccer manifest themselves in the banners and signage displayed at the games themselves. In August of 2017, Poland's Legia Warsaw hosted FC Astana, from Kazakhstan, in a UEFA Champions League qualifying match. The game took place on the anniversary of the 1944 Warsaw Uprising, when Polish resistance fighters sought to retake the city from the Nazi forces controlling it. The tifo took up one of the entire stands of Legia Warsaw's home ground, Polish Army Stadium, and featured as a backdrop a Polish flag with the year "1944" superimposed over it. In front of that stood a German officer, his face unseen, holding his pistol to the head of a frightened child. Across the bottom of the stand ran a message in English: "During the Warsaw Uprising Germans killed 160,000 people. Thousands of them were children."[2]

UEFA, the governing body for European soccer, reacted to this about as well as you might have thought, and fined the team €35,000 for their choice of tifo.[3] Legia Warsaw, who are known for their ornate and sometimes pyrotechnically-minded tifo, responded to UEFA's fine with a tifo mocking them—including an illustration of a massive pig. It was displayed before their next European competition, later in the month. UEFA fined them €50,000 for that one.

* * *

The United States has not been immune to controversies around tifo and flags displayed by supporters. This came to a head in 2019, when the league initiated a new system of regulations centered around speech and attire in Major League Soccer stadiums. This, in turn, led stadium security personnel to confiscate flags from several supporters groups that included an Iron Front symbol[4]—a symbol with roots in anti-fascist, anti-Stalinist organization in 1930s Germany.

The league received an abundance of pushback from this, as some supporters groups who hadn't previously flown Iron Front banners chose to do so. This also led to unexpected alliances between groups that had previously clashed—including groups supporting longtime rivals Seattle Sounders and Portland Timbers. The result was a promise from the league's management to revisit the contentious policies. For their part, the USL—which governs several lower division soccer leagues across the United States and Canada—opted to let each team's management decide for themselves how they wanted to regulate (or not regulate) political speech at games.[5]

I'm not exactly a disinterested party here: I'm a longtime supporter of MLS team New York Red Bulls, and have been a dues-paying member of Empire Supporters Club for several years. ESC was founded with the goal of preventing right-wing supporters from getting a foothold in the then-nascent team;[6] its politics are crucial to its history. At Red Bulls home games, I've seen political displays from ESC's section; I also saw, albeit briefly, someone hold up a Blue Lives Matter flag elsewhere in the stadium. There are also a couple of banners discussing religion if you look hard enough. All of that doesn't seem contradictory to me; instead, it reflects a team with an ideologically diverse fanbase. But in the context of a team that also holds Pride Night celebrations and has a few designated gender-neutral bathrooms in their stadium, it seems surreal to argue that stating an opposition to fascists is beyond the pale when certain other steps—which do resonate politically in the present-day United States—aren't.

* * *

All of which comes to what may be the most ubiquitous of political signs at a sporting event. It's ubiquitous, and it's visible in all sports, from football to American football to arena football. As signage goes, it's also particularly terse: one word and two numbers in length. That would be "John 3:16," a piece of signage with a surreal history and with dimensions far beyond the theological.

On the surface of things, this reference to a Bible verse isn't terribly political; rather, there are Bible quotes that are far more politically charged. And to simply state one's Christianity is not an inherently political act: as is the case with literally any belief system, Christianity has its liberal adherents and its conservative ones, its moderates and its apolitical types. And John 3:16 is not, on the face of it, a political statement. "For God so loved the world, that he gave his only begotten Son, that whosoever believeth in him should not perish, but have eternal life," it reads—a relatively uncontroversial statement for someone identifying as a Christian to stand by.

With these signs, however, it's less about the message itself and more about how it's been deployed. At the heart of the initial movement to hang the banner in stadiums was a man named Rollen Stewart, whom *The New York Times* described in a 1985 article as "an itinerant evangelist who can often be seen at sporting events wearing a bushy, rainbow-striped wig and a T-shirt carrying a John 3:16 reference."[7] He was initially known as a colorful figure who might pop up on sports broadcasts: the wig and his penchant for dancing made him a hard person to miss.

Soon enough, he added a religious component to his persona. After forays into an acting career and a marijuana farming business, Stewart decided to pledge his life to spreading the Gospel, adding a reference to it to his attire and beginning to carry signage with the verse emblazoned on it.[8] For some in the sporting world, he was a friendly or reassuring sight; for others, he was a point of conflict.

In 1984, Stewart and a man named Stephen Francis sought to hang "John 3:16" banners at Washington, DC's

Robert F. Kennedy Stadium during NFL games. Security personnel asked them to remove the banner; the following year, Stewart and Francis filed a lawsuit. They didn't go it alone, however—providing legal advice was a group called the Rutherford Institute,[9] who have spent several decades working on various civil liberties-related causes. Trying to pin down their politics isn't easy; if pressed, I'd fall back on the catch-all "libertarian." Stewart emerged victorious in his case[10]—likely one of the reasons religious signage continues to appear at stadiums around the country.

Here's where things take a turn for the explicitly political. John 3:16 as a work of signage began to gain conservative credibility. In 2009, a young quarterback named Tim Tebow drew abundant media attention when playing for the University of Florida. And as Tebow accrued fame for his skills on the gridiron, he also attracted plenty of attention for his espousal of a conservative variety of Christianity. Tebow often wrote "John 3:16" in the eye black he wore in games— and, as writer Monte Burke at *Forbes* noted, Tebow's high-profile gestures seemed to act as a jumpstart to other similar professions of faith at sporting events.[11]

While "John 3:16" may be apolitical, Tebow himself is far from it. In 2010, he appeared in an anti-abortion Super Bowl advertisement from the conservative organization Focus on the Family.[12] He was rumored to be appearing at the 2016 Republican National Convention, only to opt out.[13] And in recent years, he's made a foray into film production; one review of his debut in that arena, *Run the Race*, pointed out that it was "unflatteringly explicit about its conservative ideology."[14] What does it mean when the preeminent advocate for a particular bit of scripture advocates right-of-center politics? The messages painted on Tebow's face ended when his NFL career began due to the league's regulations,[15] but his position in popular culture was assured.

Following their Super Bowl ad with Tebow in 2010, Focus on the Family opted to make use of John 3:16 in their advertisement for the same game two years later. The ad featured a group of children reciting the Bible verse; broadcaster CBS attracted some criticism for airing it, as Fox had turned down a similar ad for the Super Bowl the previous year.[16] And Focus on the Family is no ordinary religious organization: They espouse a version of Christianity that lines up with very conservative political positions, including opposition to abortion and marriage equality. And they doubled down on, effectively, ownership of John 3:16—adding a distinctly political cast to a verse that can nominally be embraced by Christians regardless of their voting habits.

In a 2018 sermon reprinted on the religion website Patheos, Rev. Adam Eriksen of the Clackamas United Church of Christ wrote about his own frustrations with John 3:16 and the ways in which it has entered popular culture. "Progressive Christians have become so familiar with this passage that we treat it with contempt. At least I do," he wrote. "Whenever I see those signs during a football game, I roll my eyes."[17]

Eriksen's piece was headlined "How Progressive Christians Can Reclaim John 3:16," and it's a theme he returns to again and again. But it's telling that he feels the need to make this distinction—again, context matters. And as of this writing, John 3:16 largely remains a tool of a conservative ideology, and its dissemination across the airwaves acts as a massive political sign all its own.

INTERLUDE: THE PUNK CHAPTER

To write about my political beliefs as unchanging feels fundamentally incorrect: as knowledge can shape ideology, so too can partisan politics have their own influence on partisan alignment. The political beliefs I hold now are not entirely the same ones I held ten or twenty years ago. That being said, there are certain issues about which I feel more strongly, others of which I was not aware before now, and others still that I thought had been settled that recent electoral developments have again put into play.

I first voted for the nation's highest office in the 1996 presidential election. At the time, the country's politics were not so different from that of our politics in 2020; in other respects, they're tremendously different. The way that I was a self-described leftist at 20 is not, perhaps, the same way that I'm a self-described leftist now. But there are certain core ideological beliefs that shaped both the person I was then and the person I am now; those beliefs have stayed relatively consistent, even as the implications of where they might lead me—and the scope of what those ideals might mean—have evolved.

All of which is a very roundabout way of saying that punk helped to shape my beliefs—and, even more so, the era in which I found myself listening to punk played a significant role in my own ideological development. Punk, Ann Nocenti's *Daredevil* run, and going to an Equal Rights Amendment rally as a small child—those were the building blocks of an overly cautious democratic socialist with a mild contrarian streak. Please get your tomatoes ready for the throwing—the more rotten the better.

There's always been a strong anti-establishment ethos to punk, and that largely manifests itself in left-wing politics. I'm speaking largely here of bands in the United States and the United Kingdom—trying to map, for example, the East German punk bands Timothy Mohr wrote about in his excellent 2018 book *Burning Down the Haus: Punk Rock, Revolution, and the Fall of the Berlin Wall* onto a right-left continuum can be a little trickier. Many iconic British and American punk bands emerged during the administrations of Margaret Thatcher and Ronald Reagan, respectively, and pushed back against the conservative politics of the time.

But by the early 1990s, punk's relationship to power had changed somewhat. Ascendant on both sides of the Atlantic was the Third Way movement, exemplified by the administrations of Tony Blair and Bill Clinton. Authoritarian conservatives continued to draw the ire of punk bands everywhere, especially given the culture-war politics demonstrated by Republican politicians beginning in the late 1980s and early 1990s. This included attacks by Republican senators Jesse Helms and Alphonse D'Amato on the National Endowment for the Arts in 1989[1] and then–Senate Majority Leader Bob Dole criticizing the film industry for depictions of violence in 1995.[2] While there have always been conservative musicians, filmmakers, and artists, this period formalized a broader ideological divide. A 2007 article by Benjamin Nugent in the journal *n + 1* had the headline "Why Don't Republicans Write Fiction?"[3] This moment in political and cultural history serves as one possible answer to that question.

But coming of age in punk amid two different forms of the Establishment—the familiar right wing and a newer center-left that seemed bound and determined to push back against any progressive policies of the past—also led to a murkier ideological space. It's what led me to vote for Ralph Nader for President twice, in 1996 and 2000, for instance. Admittedly, I cast one as a resident of New Jersey and one as a resident of New York, fully aware of the protest-vote qualities of each and the relative safety of voicing each of those protests. But embracing punk in the United States during the Clinton presidency had, I'd argue, some ideological quirks that might not have been as true for someone who got into punk when Reagan or Bush was president.

Certain punk bands have walked a fine line in terms of criticizing authorities on the left while still maintaining their own leftist politics. Probably the most searing example of this is the 1979 Dead Kennedys song "California Über Alles," which criticized the (first) gubernatorial reign of Democrat Jerry Brown. A memorable 1992 cover by the Disposable Heroes of Hiphoprisy notably updated the lyrics to be about conservative Republican Pete Wilson. The Dead Kennedys soon turned their satirical scorn on the Reagan administration, but they also established a larger context for challenging power dynamics, even when they didn't fall along expected lines.

The Dead Kennedys also provided another lens by which I could explore political signs. The cover artwork to some of the genre's most formative albums also serve as political signage, and the unsettling political collages found on many a Dead Kennedys album cover, courtesy of the artist Winston Smith, certainly fit into that category. Smith's artwork juxtaposed traditionally patriotic or jingoistic images with unsettling, horrific ones, making for a harrowing critique of then-contemporary American politics. One of Smith's pieces, for the Dead Kennedys' *Give Me Convenience or Give Me Death*, features a mother bottle-feeding a baby—but in this case the bottle has been swapped out for a missile. Below it sits the piece's title: "Force-Fed War."

John Yates, an artist and record label owner, adopted a similar aesthetic for the work that he did under the Stealworks banner and during his tenure running the label Allied Records. If Smith's art tended toward the grotesque, Yates's was more ironic, creating a more implicit contrast between the cheerily patriotic images in his artwork and the politically charged sentiments found on the music within. Some of Yates's work memorably finds its way into a nostalgic vein, only to subvert that feeling with a subtler detail. His cover artwork for an audio version of Howard Zinn's *A People's History of the United States* features an outline of the United States overlaid with the stars and stripes; the mood is deeply retro-patriotic, right up until the point where you notice the drops of red that look like uncannily like bloodstains.

The same can be said for countless politically minded groups, including the British anarchopunk group Crass, whose albums used stark collages and juxtapositions of inspirational slogans with horrific imagery to criticize the Thatcher government. Politically minded hip-hop groups like Public Enemy, dead prez, and The Coup also used their albums' artwork to critique economic and racial inequality in American society.

All of which is to say that, while having punk soundtrack large chunks of my formative years certainly impacted the way I look at politics, it also served as a rough education in some of the same visual concepts and themes I'd later find elsewhere in the world of political signs. That's not tremendously surprising, as subcultures can echo the larger culture in unexpected ways. But it's one more way in which political signs are more than simply banners touting a candidate or issue.

11 KNIVES BATS NEW (POLITICAL) TATS

You wouldn't expect the most prominent political tattoo in the United States to be found on the body of a conservative man in his late sixties, but reality sometimes has a penchant for the unexpected. Witness, then, the back of Roger Stone: onetime Richard M. Nixon associate, a pioneer in the art of lobbying Congress, and a collaborator with Julian Assange of WikiLeaks—actions which led to his arrest in early 2019. It can be argued that Roger Stone bridges nearly fifty years of Republican Party history, from Richard Nixon to Donald Trump. How you feel about that—and whether you see Stone as something closer to a hero or a villain—likely depends upon your feelings on said political party.

Besides his long political career, Roger Stone is chiefly known for one other thing: a massive tattoo of Richard M. Nixon's face located on his back. In a 2008 profile of Stone for *The New Yorker*, Jeffrey Toobin touched upon the origins of Stone's distinctive tattoo. (The article included a photograph of a shirtless Stone—regrettably, it only showed him from the front.) Toobin posited the tattoo as a means of contrasting Stone with some of his cohorts on the right—a fair point of comparison.

> Although Stone shares many of Nixon's resentments, his own tastes have always tended to more Rabelaisian pleasures than "champagne music" and Salisbury steak. Not long ago, Stone went to the Ink Monkey tattoo shop in Venice Beach and had a portrait of Nixon's face applied to his back, right below the neck. "Women love it," Stone said.[1]

Hyperbole or not, Stone's penchant for his political mentor's face on his back is the tip of the iceberg as far as political tattoos are concerned. A quick search online turns up plenty of presidential tattoos, including iconography associated with the Obama and Trump campaigns.

But some political tattoos go beyond that, into the realm of the unexpected. In 2013, when Margaret Thatcher's funeral procession filled the streets of London, a number of news photographers caught sight of an unlikely mourner. A man with long greying hair and a white beard, clad in a long coat and what seemed to be Doc Martens,[2] stood with the crowds but looked much more like an alumnus of one of the anarchopunk bands that arose in firey response to Thatcher's politics.

Appearances can be deceiving. This man, who gave his name to reporters as Dave,[3] had a tattoo memorializing

Thatcher on his lower leg featuring a skull and crossbones, the years of Thatcher's birth and death, and the slogan "She Never Turned" above the design. It's one of the most punk rock designs imaginable used to commemorate one of the least punk rock people imaginable.

* * *

And then there's the story of the guy who did seventy-eight free Donald Trump–themed tattoos in the span of a year.[4] Bob Holmes, owner of The Clay Dragon Tattoo Studio in Seabrook, New Hampshire, offered to give a Trump-themed tattoo to anyone who asked for it within one year. Seventy-eight people took him up on his offer—some local, some from across the country, according to an article in The Daily Beast.[5]

The selection of tattoos pictured offer a good cross-section of what the state of political tattoos in early twenty-first-century America look like. Some are pretty straightforward: Trump's last name, or the slogan "Make America Great Again." Another is more fanciful: Donald Trump, clad in a button-down shirt, jacket, and tie, tearing the shirt open to reveal a Superman-style "T" underneath.[6]

Some of the images in Holmes's portfolio read like the tattoo editions of political signage you might see elsewhere as part of a campaign. That's not confined to Trump, either; a quick image search reveals numerous tattoo variations on Shepard Fairey's "HOPE" image for Barack Obama's 2008 campaign. And some opt for flattering portraits of their subjects: A search on the photo-sharing site Flickr led me to a man who got what appears to be a detailed image of Ralph Nader's face tattooed on one of his forearms.[7]

But elsewhere, things get weirder, more personal. Political tattoos can combine the ephemerality of political signage with the enduring power of ink etched into your skin—but they can also combine elements in a way that says plenty about the idiosyncrasies of the person being tattooed.

*　　*　　*

Soccer is full of larger-than-life figures, perhaps none more so than the Argentinian legend Diego Maradona. His playing career spanned three decades and involved one of the most controversial goals in the history of the game. But Maradona is known for his outsized personality as much as (if not more than) his abilities as a player. Maradona's politics are very much on the left-wing side of the political spectrum, and his choice of tattoos reflects that.

"It was time that the two greatest Argentines were united in the same body," he said of his tattoo of Che Guevara.[8] That's not his only political tattoo; there's also one of Fidel Castro on his leg. In a 2007 interview, he spoke about wanting to get a third political leader's image tattooed on his body: Venezuela's Hugo Chavez.[9] Another athlete who did get a Chavez tattoo was boxer Edwin Valero—in this case, across his chest. Unfortunately, Valero is probably best known for his actions outside of the boxing ring: He repeatedly abused his wife, then died by suicide after being arrested for her murder.[10]

Other athletes have also opted to get tattoos reflecting their political beliefs. In 2017, Washington Wizards point guard John Wall had a Black Power symbol tattooed on his back, joining several other images related to the civil rights movement.[11]

*　*　*

All of the above begs the question: Just what constitutes a political tattoo? Does it have to be a recognizable political figure, or can it be something more abstract? One of the mediums that Doreen Garner, an artist based in Philadelphia, works in is tattooing; a 2018 article about her residency at the Brooklyn art space Pioneer Works talked about the pop-up tattoo parlor that she established there. Garner's work is often politically charged—among the art on display at Pioneer Works was a statue evoking the medical experiments carried out on black women by J. Marion Sims in the nineteenth century.

> The growing library of tattoos Garner draws from for the project includes black panther heads, cotton flowers, and portraits of Martin Luther King Jr. and Angela Davis. A unique pricing structure is built in: Those who self-identify as black or brown people of color can receive select tattoos free of charge.[12]

Part of Garner's work also deals with representation in the tattoo world, in which most of the artists are white men.

Her growing prominence in this scene is a way to push back against it—and to adorn bodies with politically resonant images as she goes.

In the interest of learning more about what might motivate someone to get a political tattoo, I talked to a few people about their own experiences and what their takes on political tattoos were. Denver resident Rachel Knaizer spoke to me about a few of her tattoos, especially one that she had created as a tribute to Supreme Court Justice Ruth Bader Ginsburg. "I have tattoos dedicated to my maternal grandparents, and was looking for ideas that would best represent my paternal grandparents and their history," she told me. "The infamous RBG reminds me a lot of my paternal grandmother: rooted in firmly held values; willing to take action on behalf of others; ready to be the voice of dissent for a greater purpose."

Knaizer mentioned that it was important for her Ginsburg-themed tattoo to be consistent with the tattoos elsewhere on her body. "A large number of my other tattoos are in the American Traditional Style, and I wanted to stay in that vein," she said. "I also wanted a slightly less apparent reference to RBG. In the end, I chose an American Traditional heart and rose design with her initials in the banner."

The location, she told me, was also critically important due to its visibility. "Occasionally, people ask why I chose to get the tattoo on the back of my thigh," she said. "I tell them that tattoos are as much about what you want to cherish and remember as what you want other people to see. I want other people to see this one and consider how legal decisions affect all of us. Of course, I can't guarantee that audience reaction."

While Knaizer's RBG tattoo is the only one of a nominally political figure it's not her only political tattoo. In our conversation she cited two others that she considered political in nature: "One is from one of Basquiat's journals that reads, 'Mona Lisa/Men have named you a second class citizen,'" she told me. "The other is from *Star Trek*, is referenced in *Station Eleven*, and sits below the RBG tattoo. It reads, 'To survive is not enough.'"

And she said that she's probably not done with seeking out more in a similar vein. "I would definitely get more politically themed tattoos," she said.

My fellow writer Mairead Case also talked with me about her experience with political tattoos—which involved a deep dive into their epistemology. "Aristotle wasn't always a cool dude but his phrase 'politikon zoon' means a social animal— an animal intended to live in a city. I like that a lot," she said. "For me political tattoos are marks reminding us of (note: this is different than committing us to) our responsibilities to and need for others. If the work I do on this planet does not connect me to others or my selves, or others to themselves, then I'm really in trouble."

Case's political tattoo draws inspiration from the artwork of David Wojnarowicz. "This one is three short, parallel lines on the outside of my right forearm. Specifically, it's after three stitches in a David Wojnarowicz painting about blood," she said when describing the subject of our conversation. "He used certain motifs pretty regularly though, so I also mean it to honor the stitches he made through bread and in that photograph of his lips. He mostly used red thread, but my marks are black, like they've been photographed."

She described the tattoo as a result of a very particular moment in her life—one that coincided with a retrospective of Wojnarowicz's work at the Whitney Museum of American Art. "I was coming out of a bad, dark time and flew my own self to New York just to sit on some stoops and see the Wojnarowicz retrospective," she said. "When I saw those stitch paintings in person I knew I'd found my mark. The thread. I walked down the street, found a shop, got it done, then went back and walked through the show again."

For Case, it's also important that this particular tattoo is political, but its meaning isn't apparent from the outset. "I like that the origin isn't obvious unless we talk about it together," she said.

As a fellow veteran of the punk scene, I asked Case if she could recall any political tattoos that she'd seen in the past that were either inspiring or cringe worthy. "Yes, some Nazi bullshit at punk shows and corner stores in Indiana, Colorado, and Illinois. Those kinds of tattoos are obviously deeper than cringe," she said. "I do have some friends with straightedge tattoos who aren't straightedge anymore, and those make us cringe-laugh. Being human is pretty funny."

The almost limitless array of images that can constitute a political tattoo makes them something of an outlier among forms of political signage. Because of a tattoo's inherent proximity to the self, it doesn't necessarily need to provide the context that so many other political signs do. Tattoos can serve as a kind of secret code, only registering as political to someone who understands their meaning. A friend of mine has Salvador Allende's last words tattooed on his shoulder; if someone familiar with Allende or the circumstances of his death sees them, their message is very clear. For someone unfamiliar with Allende and no knowledge of Spanish, the impact will be far less.

But that makes sense. Tattoos are a singular gesture; in their platonic ideal, they should be something sincere and deeply personal. It's not surprising that a person's tattoo (or tattoos) would reflect their deeply held political beliefs— but it's also not surprising that those tattoos might take a less obvious route toward declaring them.

The question of what makes a political tattoo a political tattoo hits close to home for me. On my left arm, just below my shoulder, I have a six-word tattoo taken from the Grant Morrison–penned comic book *The Invisibles*. Specifically, it's the last six words that appear in the comic—a comic that is nothing if not deeply political, featuring sinister conspiracies, authoritarian villains, and a prominent set piece involving the legacy of the Spanish Civil War.

We made gods and jailers because we felt small and ashamed and alone. We let them try us and judge us and, like sheep to slaughter, we allowed ourselves to be sentenced. See! Now! Our sentence is up.[13]

I hadn't necessarily thought of my "See! Now! Our sentence is up." tattoo as a political symbol; over the course of assembling this chapter, though, it's hard to think of it as anything else.

12 HOPE AND ITS DISCONTENTS

It was a warm July morning and I was sitting in the Monmouth County Historical Association's research room, folders and documents before me. I was there to poke and prod my way into local history, to see what signs of bygone campaigns I could find, both on the local and national levels. What did I see? Tickets to a Policeman's Ball; a mailer from a local Republican candidate depicting a donkey wearing an apron and badly mixing a punchbowl; municipal newsletters from the 1960s and their counterparts from a few decades later, when layout skills had deprecated dramatically over the years.

It was with two national campaigns' ephemera that I recognized something very particular. (*Ephemera* might be too formal of a word for these particular items. They were bumper stickers, about as utilitarian as it gets.) The first was for the Bush/Quayle ticket in 1992: a red, white, and blue color scheme; the name "Bush" on one line and the name "Quayle" on the line below it, the text of equal size. The largest font was reserved for the "'92" at the very end of the bumper sticker.

The second was for the Clinton/Gore ticket four years later. This also had a red, white, and blue color scheme; here, too, the name Clinton was directly above the name Gore, and the sizes of each name were equal. For this bumper sticker, the "'96" was the largest object by far.

Imagine someone with no knowledge whatsoever of late-twentieth-century American politics. This hypothetical person, whether raised on an island or traveling through time, comes across these two stickers. What can they learn from them? The candidates' names; the years in which the elections occurred. Perhaps if they were feeling up for a leap, they would successfully guess the colors of the flag of the nation in which these candidates were running for office. And that's all.

There's no mention of political parties on these signs, no inkling of either ticket's proposed policies—just two names and a year; the context surrounding the rest is supplied by whoever's taking in the sticker. A dedicated Republican might cheer the name of George Bush; a Third Wave Democrat might smile wistfully as they recall Bill Clinton's time in office. A diehard supporter of Ross Perot, Gary Johnson, Jill Stein, or Ralph Nader might find both stickers entirely distasteful and could even, perhaps, be overtaken by the urge to scrape one such sticker from the bumper of a car on which it was affixed, crumple it up, and discard it—going on to carve a message into the underlying paint decrying the prevalence of the two-party system in American politics over the last century and a half. Or perhaps not.

* * *

Staring down at these two bumper stickers, each supporting an incumbent running for re-election for the nation's highest office, what struck me the most was this: neither one looked remotely partisan. If there's a Republican Party or a Democratic Party means of designing bumper stickers—or a Green or Libertarian or Reform Party method of the same—it was apparent in neither of these cases.

Times have changed.

Barack Obama's candidacy in 2008 was a seismic one for American politics. One of the defining symbols of that candidacy was artist Shepard Fairey's portrait of the future president: a stylized image of Obama's face, colored mostly blue with some red accents, and the word HOPE. It established an aesthetic, and many variations on this design manifested as bumper stickers, posters, and flyers.

Eight years later, Donald Trump's presidential candidacy proved seismic for entirely different reasons. Trump's campaign also had an indelible object associated with it: in this case, a red baseball cap emblazoned with the slogan MAKE AMERICA GREAT AGAIN. It became visual shorthand for its candidate's run for office; MAGA is now verbal shorthand for the ideology of Trump and many of his supporters.

But candidates have always had distinctive items of memorabilia: I can remember uncovering my maternal grandmother's I LIKE IKE pin, for instance. Plenty of candidates have had distinctly designed imagery, have had caps, shirts, or other articles of clothing made, that's certainly true. But I'd argue that where these objects differ from their predecessors is the way they're coded. Someone with no knowledge of the candidates might pick up a Clinton/Gore '96 bumper sticker and have no idea about their ideology. A glimpse of a MAGA hat or a HOPE poster is far more telling.

Start with the colors. In 2000, American election results began to use red for states won by Republicans and blue for states won by Democrats. Not long after that, we got red states and blue states; not long after that, they entered the cultural lexicon. Filmmaker Kevin Smith made a horror film titled *Red State*; comedian Colin Quinn debuted a one-man show titled *Red State Blue State*. Four years before his run for President, Barack Obama memorably addressed the 2004 Democratic National Convention with a speech that, in part, endeavored to undermine the stereotypes associated with states both blue and red. The relevant passage went like this:

> The pundits, the pundits like to slice-and-dice our country into Red States and Blue States; Red States for Republicans, Blue States for Democrats. But I've got news for them, too. We worship an awesome God in the Blue States, and we don't like federal agents poking around in our libraries in the Red States. We coach Little League in the Blue States and yes, we've got some gay friends in the Red States.[1]

Whether or not it worked will be left for future historians to decide, unless we've permanently ruined civilization. Even then, perhaps evolved dolphins will figure it out or something.

The tricky thing about talking red states and blue states is this: it lines up too neatly with the increased partisanship of American politics—which lines up too neatly with the ways in which the worst aspects of American partisanship echo the worst aspects of sports fandom.

Red/blue rivalries don't just show up every four years on an electoral map. If you've spent any time at all watching Premier League soccer—I write this as a founding member of Brooklyn Spurs, thank you very much—you might have noticed something about some of the most heated intracity rivalries—say, Liverpool and Everton, or Manchester United and Manchester City, or Arsenal and Tottenham Hotspur. One team is traditionally associated with the color red, and one team with the color blue. The same is also true for a soccer rivalry closer to home for me here on the other side of the Atlantic: the New York Red Bulls and New York City Football Club also slide neatly into the red/blue dynamic.

To put it more simply, red and blue aren't just coded for partisan purposes: they're literally the colors of your team.

The cool blue hues of Shepard Fairey's Obama portrait are a pretty significant hat-tip to the politics of the man it pictures. And Fairey's own distinctive style and roots in the world of street art lend the image far more cultural cachet than any comparable candidate dating back to John F.

Kennedy. The Make America Great Again hat is resolutely uncool: it holds no secret knowledge of fonts or kerning and is unlikely to break any new aesthetic ground. (Both designs have lent themselves well to parody, but that's not quite the same thing.) And its coloration is the platonic ideal of red.

(As an aside: Just how a color previously associated with Communism became associated with a political party with an unrestrained embrace of free markets falls neatly into the realm of historical ironies. But then again, the worlds of political signage and political messaging abound with strange and surreal ironies.)

Remove all context from most American political signage throughout history and you're left with a series of names, virtually interchangeable—but not so for Obama and HOPE, not so for Trump and MAGA. The timing may have also been right for these two campaigns. In his 2014 book *Curationism: How Curating Took Over the Art World and Everything Else*, critic and editor David Balzer explored the rise of "curate" as a term and what its broader implications are for society. An early passage is particularly relevant when considering political identity.

I contend that, since about the mid-1990s, we have been living in the curationist moment, in which institutions and businesses rely on others, often variously credentialed experts, to cultivate and organize things in an expression-cum-assurance of value and an attempt to make affiliations with, and to court, various audiences and consumers. As these audiences and consumers, we are engaged as well, cultivating and organizing our identities duly, as we are prompted.[2]

Wearing some element of political signage—or hanging a HOPE poster on a wall—seems as pronounced a way of "cultivating and organizing our identities" as one could imagine.

*   *   *

For a glimpse at what campaign signage wholly untethered from past expectations might resemble, an art exhibit that appeared at the Visual Arts Gallery in New York City in the first half of 2012 might be instructive. The exhibit, titled *Re Elect*, was the brainchild of artist and designer Kevin O'Callaghan, who teaches at the School of Visual Arts. As Steven Heller, O'Callaghan's SVA colleague, described it for *The Atlantic*, the result involved a series of installations offering a contemporary take on what might happen if former presidents ran for office again.

> For *Re Elect*, [O'Callaghan] provided each student with a pre-constructed podium on a platform, a 15-foot-high wall with nothing on it, and the name of a president. The students' responsibility was to use the podium as a major or minor element in their design, fill the background with a strong, two- or three-dimensional image, and otherwise have free reign on how they metaphorically caricatured or illustrated their respective candidates.[3]

For designer Jennifer Rozbruch, who was tasked with working on Gerald Ford's theoretical campaign, this involved signage touting his athletic prowess early in life. The pinnacle of her display is a sign for Ford's 1976 campaign with the slogan "A Successful Interception," a nod to his unique status as the only American president to have reached that position without ever being elected. "This campaign underscores Ford's strengths as a football player, and uses this theme to highlight his often forgotten accomplishments in the White House: intercepting a national nightmare and allowing the country to heal," Rozbruch wrote about her work.[4]

The poster for the exhibit made use of an effortlessly timeless design, evoking both psychedelic artwork of the 1960s and the intersecting arcs found upon closer inspection of currency. Several presidents—among them Ronald Reagan, John F. Kennedy, and Theodore Roosevelt—were prominently featured on the center in black and white, along with the phrase "RE-ELECT."[5] The effect was not unlike something taken out of time, both archaic and a suitable descendent of Shepard Fairey's irreverent street-art roots.

*   *   *

The stylistic influences of the Obama 2008 and Trump 2016 campaigns have spread far beyond their original campaign roots. In her memoir *Names for the Sea: Strangers in Iceland*, Sarah Moss describes a year spent teaching in Reykjavik and of witnessing the 2009 protests over the governmental corruption that led to the nation's economic collapse. The protest Moss described lined up with another political event taking place across the Atlantic, and the convergence of the two led to one particularly serendipitous moment.

> The crowd grew. It was the day of President Barack Obama's inauguration in the US, and Icelandic protestors had banners saying, "Yes, we can!"[6]

Fairey's iconic design for the Obama campaign led to aesthetic successors on both sides of the American political divide. And to be fair, he wasn't the only artist who created a distinctive poster for a candidate seeking the Democratic presidential nomination in 2008. Artist and writer Tony Puryear[7] created a poster based on a Bryan Adams photograph[8] in which a turtleneck-clad Clinton gazes off into the distance. The background evokes the stripes of the American flag waving in the wind, while the name HILLARY occupies the bottom of the image.

For my money, Puryear's image has an understated elegance to it; I'd argue that it's more compelling than most of the signage from Clinton's campaign eight years later. In a reprise of his work for Clinton's rival in 2008, Shepard Fairey came up with a design for Bernie Sanders's campaign for the Democratic nomination. In this case, it came in the form of a T-shirt bearing Sanders's name and a torch-carrying arm evoking the Statue of Liberty; the phrase "Feel the Bern" can be seen as well.[9]

In an interview with CNN around the election, the artist discussed why he hadn't ever created a design featuring Clinton the way he had Obama or Sanders. He responded that he "found her inspiring enough," though he was clear about his feelings on who to vote for in the general election. "I think Hillary Clinton is much better for the United States than Donald Trump," Fairey said.[10] Fairey also discussed a print he had made of Donald Trump, which focuses on his contorted mouth, and served as artwork for the Franz Ferdinand song "Demagogue."[11]

In the same interview, Fairey spoke about the influence another stylized portrait of a president had had on his development as an artist: Robbie Conal's *Contra Diction*. "I thought it has got a sense of humor, it's saying something politically and the portrait of Reagan is a great painting, though it's unflattering," Fairey told CNN.[12]

Contra Diction features an image of Ronald Reagan at its center, with "Contra" above him and "Diction" below. The image of the former president is deeply unflattering, giving him the look of an undead creature from a 1930s horror film[13]—it's one of many politically charged images he's created over the years. And a 1995 *Washington Post* article chronicles how he spent a night blanketing Washington, DC with images of Newt Gingrich captioned "NEWT/WIT."[14]

More recently, Conal has brought his vision to bear on the Trump administration, with images of various officials and hangers-on rendered in his distinctive style. In a 2018 interview with Artnow LA that billed him as "The Godfather of Guerilla Poster Artists," Conal commented on his methods of distribution: "If you're making art about public issues that you really care about without figuring a way to distribute it to the public doesn't work."[15] It's a statement of purpose that could apply to plenty of political signage found around the world.

*   *   *

Donald Trump's unlikely ascent to the presidency brought with it a host of strange juxtapositions, bizarre political comebacks, and surreal aesthetics. Near the top of any list of the bizarre side effects of Trump's election would be the spotlight it turned on the street artist Sabo: The headline for a 2017 *The Guardian* article on Sabo posed the question, "Is this artist the rightwing Banksy?"[16] And if the concept of a right-wing Banksy seems strange to you, well—that's just the beginning.

Sabo first became the subject of political think pieces in 2015, when his enthusiasm for Senator Ted Cruz led him to create an image of a shirtless, heavily tattooed, impressively muscled Cruz smoking a cigarette. A 2015 *Washington Post* article by Katie Zezima described the origin of the image, which had become a huge hit at that year's Conservative Political Action Conference.

Sabo says he felt as though his right-leaning views were under attack in Los Angeles, and was intrigued by Cruz.

Inspired by a friend who superimposed tattoos onto depictions of Marilyn Monroe's body, he created the image and plastered it around his city.[17]

Despite the cognitive dissonance of the famously buttoned-down Cruz looking like something out of Nicholas Winding Refn's crime epic *Bronson*, it's not difficult to see why conservatives would latch on to this. Like it or not, rebellion has always had plenty of cool cachet; conservatives, who tend to represent the capital-e Establishment, are generally not the heroes of youth-in-revolt storylines. (I'm not going to cite *Footloose* here, but I'm not not going to cite it either, if you get my drift.) And as someone who lived through the brief moment in the late '90s when people tried to make conservative punk a thing—because rebelling against punk rock was the *real* punk rock, man—it's not hard to see why the conservative establishment wouldn't embrace an irreverent, unpredictable artist prone to going off-message and speaking without a filter.

Shortly before Election Day 2016, Sabo told CNN that he had decided to vote for Donald Trump.[18] Given Sabo's fondness for Ted Cruz—whose father, you may recall, Trump attempted to tie to John F. Kennedy's assassination—that hesitance is understandable. Before long, Sabo was anticipating a path for many Never Trump conservatives, moving from a reluctant vote to a wholesale embrace of the man. An interview with Rory Carroll (no relation) in *The Guardian* a year later found Sabo spreading images of a blissed-out Trump in a modified version of the lotus position, flipping everyone the double bird, all over Los Angeles.[19] As for the artist behind it, he also seemed ready to re-wage the culture wars of old, telling *The Guardian* that "I think leftism is a mental disorder."

Besides his images of Trump and Cruz, Sabo also created unflattering images of Obama, Sanders, and Gwyneth Paltrow—the last of those due to Paltrow having hosted a fundraising event that Obama attended.[20] He's also drawn criticism for use of a certain racial slur in his artwork;[21] meanwhile, the *Washington Post* article about his visit to CPAC describes him as wearing a shirt that managed to be simultaneously Islamophobic and homophobic.[22] In his 2017 interview with *The Guardian*, Sabo argued that "Republicans are the new punk."[23] This suggests a very broad definition of the word "punk"—potentially broad enough to be meaningless. And here, the surreal becomes the catastrophic at the drop of a hat.

13 WHEN ART IS A SIGN

At the most basic level, political signage and art have always had a symbiotic relationship. Before the era of widespread photographic reproduction, illustrations of candidates were frequently used on posters and signs for particular campaigns. A poster for Ulysses S. Grant's 1872 re-election campaign featured heroic illustrations of Grant and his running mate Henry Wilson as, respectively, a tanner and shoemaker:[1] The two stand heroically, clad in clothing appropriate to their professions; the effect is not unlike a temporal echo of Soviet-era socialist realism.

Other political posters hearkened back to an even earlier era of art. The Democratic ticket of Walter Mondale and Geraldine Ferraro did just that in their 1984 run for the Oval Office. Among their signage was a poster on which a design referred to Eugène Delacroix's 1830 painting *Liberty Leading the People*.[2] Delacroix's painting channeled several decades of French revolutionary fervor, and depicted a woman carrying the tricolor flag and leading a group of revolutionaries onward.

The Mondale/Ferraro poster placed Ferraro at the center: wearing a gown (a more modest choice of attire than the incongruously topless figure in Delacroix's painting) and holding an American flag, she stands elevated above the figures in the rest of the poster—including a woman prostrating herself at Ferraro's feet and Mondale himself, carrying a rifle on which a banner waves, advocating on behalf of the Equal Rights Amendment. "It's not the most direct way to advertise the Mondale-Ferraro ticket," Susan Carlson of the International Center of Photography told me, "but it attempts to position their candidacy in terms of historical, global struggles."

From an aesthetic perspective, it's a fascinating update to a storied and politically charged work of art. From a political perspective, it wasn't quite as successful: Mondale and Ferraro were unable to unseat the incumbent ticket of Ronald Reagan and George H.W. Bush.

Among the more bizarre convergences of political signage with art came in 1972, when the Democratic Party asked Andy Warhol to contribute something to George McGovern's presidential campaign[3] against incumbent Richard Nixon. The result was *Vote McGovern 84*, an edition of 250 screenprints[4] of Richard Nixon's face with "Vote McGovern" hand-lettered below it. It's in the coloration of Nixon's face that Warhol's aesthetic really comes into its own: He lends a demonic glow to Nixon's eyes and adds an apocalyptic tincture to the background, making Nixon resemble a sinister figure rising from some hellish backdrop. It's not the subtlest of critiques, but it makes its point.

It was also a work of art that Warhol came to regret. In the November 3, 1983 entry in *The Andy Warhol Diaries*, Warhol had cause to revisit the work when writing about a possible meeting with actress and writer Brooke Hayward.

> And anyway, I hate her because I keep on remembering that it was her and Jean Stein that got me in all this IRS trouble because they're the ones that asked me to do a McGovern poster, and I wanted to do something clever, so I got that bright idea to do a green face of Nixon with "Vote McGovern" under it. And that's when the IRS got so interested in me.[5]

Nixon may have been out of office for a decade at that time, but his influence—uncannily—lingered.

* * *

What happens when a political sign is grounds for horror? In 2019, an adaptation of the children's horror series *Scary Stories to Tell in the Dark* from director André Øvredal and producer Guillermo del Toro reached theaters to generally positive, albeit lukewarm, reviews. Writing about the film for the news site Vox, Aja Romano's review noted an unexpected addition to the stories' penchant for body horror, strange creatures, and relentlessly uncanny beings.

"One of the first things you see in the new tween horror film *Scary Stories To Tell In the Dark* is a row of swastikas," Romano wrote. "Plastered over a series of campaign posters for Richard Nixon, they flutter in front of the camera for a few moments, an apparent attempt to reset whatever expectations viewers may have for this film, ostensibly an adaptation of Alvin Schwartz's classic children's book trilogy."[6]

The film is a period piece—specifically, a period piece that places the supernatural activities that the film's heroes must grapple with against the backdrop of the 1968 presidential election. Did the juxtaposition work? As SYFY Wire critic James Grebey phrased it, that aesthetic choice "reads more as an allusion to the current political climate than it does as a reflection of the Milly Valley residents' views on him."[7] Alternately, as Grebey argues, it means that a film nominally set in 1968 is far more about the United States during the Trump presidency than it lets on.

One of the most unsettling uses of a political poster in the context of a horror story came via the cover of a 1980s comic book. During its long run from DC Comics' Vertigo imprint, *John Constantine: Hellblazer* featured stories written by an impressive array of authors, including Neil Gaiman, Warren Ellis, Brian Azzarello, and Garth Ennis. The series followed the title character, a magician from a working-class background, as he dealt with supernatural creatures and even nastier human adversaries; it was the sort of comic that could accommodate everything from a gut-wrenching (and non-supernatural) crime fiction arc to a scene in which Constantine tricks the devil with a clever bit of misdirection.

As befits its title character's working-class roots, the comic was also unapologetically political. Writing for *The New Inquiry* in 2013, Ken Chen chronicled the comic's origins, observing that "John Constantine is probably the only mainstream comics character deliberately designed as a fusion of counterculture and leftist politics."[8]

Chen cites the comic's origins during Margaret Thatcher's time as Prime Minister, and writes that Jamie Delano, who wrote the first forty issues of the comic, "wrote *Hellblazer* as a left-wing political diary. In Delano's *Hellblazer*, yuppies literally are demons."[9] That aesthetic comes to the forefront as Chen recalls his own experience reading the comic when it was first released.

> When I began reading *Hellblazer* as a teenager, it was the only comic that I felt uncomfortable reading on public transportation. I was worried that bystanders would see me looking at these violent, hideous images, but re-reading Delano's run, it seems unmistakably about forcing the reader to go from being a voyeur of genre horror comics and to become a witness of her own terrifying political conscience.[10]

The third issue of *Hellblazer*, dated March 1988,[11] features cover artwork by Dave McKean. In it, Constantine stands in front of a wall on which a series of posters have been pasted.

He wears a trench coat and smokes a cigarette; the look on his face is one of barely suppressed anger, and he glares out from the page at the reader.

On the wall behind him, traces of posters and graffiti are visible. An altered sign reads "Voting Tory Can Damage Your Health"; a faded poster reads "Marxism" but the rest of its message is covered up. A film schedule on the lower left-hand corner advertises showtimes for *Jesus Christ Superstar* and *Rocky Horror Picture Show*.

And there, just to the right of Constantine's back, is the most terrifying image of all: a stencil of Thatcher's face, between three and four feet in height, altered in one fundamental way. Her mouth now houses long, jagged teeth like some deep-sea fish, and a reddish gleam in her eyes echoes the setting sun in the distance. In the form of a fictional poster, *Hellblazer* wore its aesthetic on its sleeve; it suggested exactly the form the horrors found on the pages within would take.

* * *

John Constantine in the era of Margaret Thatcher wasn't the only instance of protest signs making their way into a comic published by one of the industry's two largest companies. Whether using protest signs to reflect the real world or showing off protests as part of an in-continuity plotline, comics in a shared universe are no stranger to political unrest. Less common are cases where a protest on the pages of a superhero comic prompt a political reaction from the real world—but that's exactly what happened in 2010 after an issue of *Captain America* was published.

The plot of the issue involved the book's heroes tracking down a right-wing extremist group. (That's the very quick version, and one which doesn't literally involve fifty years' worth of continuity.) One scene involved a protest in which certain signs were visible—including one reading "Stop the Socialists."[12] For anyone familiar with the Tea Party movement during Barack Obama's presidency, the scene was a familiar one. But it may have been too familiar for some: another sign in the panel featured the slogan "Tea Bag the Libs Before They Tea Bag YOU!" This, in turn, led a number of conservative news outlets to object, citing bias and objecting to the sign seemingly identifying the fictional protestors as part of a real movement.[13]

Both Brubaker, who wrote the issue, and Marvel's then–Editor-in-Chief Joe Quesada, blamed the issue on a production problem.[14] Quesada's defense was that the signs' text was taken from actual protest signs with the intention of changing them; the actual changes were lost in the proverbial shuffle.[15] He also said that the text would be changed in the future, but when one looks at the digital version of this issue now, that sign does bear a different message—the more generic "AmeriCAN Not AmericCAN'T." Whether that left anyone involved satisfied remains unknown.

14 WHEN A SIGN IS ART

What happens when political signage becomes art? In 2017, in the midst of a book tour with friend and fellow writer Duncan B. Barlow, we stopped in Minneapolis for a reading at Moon Palace Books. Our plan was to visit the traveling exhibit of Guillermo del Toro's collection of horror props, paintings, and ephemera the following day, as it was on display at the nearby Minneapolis Institute of Art. The friends we were staying with suggested that we visit another show while we were there: a curated exhibit of photographs titled *Resistance, Protest, Resilience*.

The show, curated by Yasufumi Nakamori, featured a cross-section of protest images from around the globe, some from the civil rights movement in the United States and others from Japan, Iran, and Canada.[1] An essay published on the museum's website to coincide with the show's debut discussed the idea of an image of protest as a kind of continuation of that protest: "The museum's founding curator of photography, Ted Hartwell, believed in the power of photography—its particular realism—to disseminate protesters' voices and viewpoints, otherwise unheard."[2]

A longer passage that follows that elucidates this concept a bit more.

> While we are surrounded by an ocean of images of today's street conflicts and protests, whether shot by a professional photographer or a bystander with an iPhone, I thought it was of utmost importance to display part of our strongest holdings in our protest exhibition.[3]

A year later, the Minneapolis Institute of Art hosted another exhibit that tied into questions of protest and politics. The museum's Cargill Gallery held a selection of artwork created as a memorial to Philando Castile,[4] who was shot and killed by a police officer after being pulled over for a nonworking brake light. After his death, people began sending his mother Valerie works of art dedicated to her son; she called the museum, and from that call the exhibit was born. An article by Jenna Ross at the *Minnesota Star Tribune* explored the genesis of the show and the range of work found there.

> The show, in the small Cargill Gallery off the museum's entrance lobby, includes portraits, videos and a ceramic sculpture of a broken heart, the word "why" patterned over its right atrium. There are protest posters, too. One, depicting a raised fist, was signed by dozens of students

after the death of the 32-year-old elementary school cafeteria supervisor they called "Mr. Phil."[5]

Resistance, Protest, Resilience is far from the only show held in an art museum that used either protest signs or images of protest signs as, effectively, works of art. Poster House's exhibit of signs from the Women's March was referenced earlier in these pages. In 2017, the James A. Michener Art Museum in Doylestown, Pennsylvania opened *A Time to Break Silence*, described as "comprising 31 works that chronicle protests, social movements, and ideological shifts since the 1950s."[6] The show took its name from Martin Luther King Jr.'s speech "Beyond Vietnam: A Time to Break Silence," and its opening commemorated the fiftieth anniversary of the speech.[7]

New York's International Center for Photography has held several shows that include signs of both protest and campaigning. 2016's *Winning the White House: From Press Prints to Selfies* and 2017's *Perpetual Revolution: The Image and Social Change* each explored questions of politics through the visual medium. And artist Jason Lazarus's ongoing *A Century of Dissent* project involves contemporary reconstructions of historical protest signs.[8]

In a 2014 article in *Frieze* about Lazarus's work, Carmen Winant wrote that "Jason Lazarus is often described as an artist activist. But it would be more apt to say that he makes work about activism. In Lazarus's hands, art is a channel through which to consider failure and attempt, desperation and motivation, abandonment and cause."[9] Lazarus has created installments of *A Century of Dissent* in both Harlem[10] and Miami,[11] and images of both installations contain handmade work that evokes both past controversies and ongoing issues in these cities. Taking this work in is a unique experience: it feels like a simulacrum of something else and a distinct entity unto itself. Am I looking at a replica of a Black Lives Matter sign or am I looking at an actual Black Lives Matter sign, to take one example—or does it matter?

Lazarus's work is also present at a moment when the boundary between art and politics—if ever it existed—has become porous. In her 2018 book *Whitewalling: Art, Race & Protest in 3 Acts*, Aruna D'Souza explored three distinct points in art history where works of art became political flashpoints. The most recent of these involved painter Dana Schutz's painting of Emmett Till's body, which appeared in the 2017 Whitney Biennial. What began as a debate over appropriation and the racial dynamics of a white artist painting the body of a black man who was murdered by white people quickly grew into a larger protest movement, and led to the creation of a number of creative and critical works.[12] Adding to the debate, a *New Yorker* profile of Schutz by Calvin Tomkins noted that the Till portrait was not really representative of Schutz's work[13]—leading to questions about why this painting was in the show at all. Since then, more museums have become the sights of protests, whether over a board member having made their fortune via immoral means or concerning frustrating aesthetic decisions.

It's the latest step in a long convergence of art and protest signs: Consider the efforts of art-world activists the Guerilla Girls, whose distinctive signage has called out the inequalities and hypocrisies of art institutions for decades. But there's also a fine-art edge to their work; they have been the subject of retrospectives in art museums in recent years. When you're taking in a Guerilla Girls retrospective, are you looking at art or a protest? Can it be both?

When I asked Melissa Walker from Poster House about the effects of putting a protest sign up in a museum and whether it changed its meaning, she replied in the affirmative. "Yes, it certainly gives gravity to the message of a poster," she said, "especially an improvised/amateur one like the ones from the march." She cited two examples that stood out to her. One was made from a pizza box, and had the phrase "Dismantle the Oligarchy" written on it. The other, she told me, contained lyrics from Tupac Shakur's "Keep Ya Head Up" written on a shopping bag.

"This small gesture by the protester of writing out something meaningful to them feels so personal, immediate, and, at that time, an expression of frustration," Walker explained. "It's nice to look back, review, and move forward with a renewed sense of purpose."

Susan Carlson, Assistant Curator at the International Center of Photography, had similarly incisive observations on the politically charged exhibits she'd worked on—and how some detachment from their original context can ultimately reveal more about them than one might expect.

"Once campaign ephemera is separated from its original purpose and immediate historic moment it can be easier to see some of the messages, intended and unintended, that campaigns put forth," she said. "It's incredible how much information is embodied in campaign materials, both information about how candidates want to position themselves and about their intended audiences."

For Walker, that shift in context can be crucial for viewers to form their own opinions about certain works of signage emerging from political campaigns. "It can also be really powerful for visitors to be able to make connections across history," she told me. "While there are certainly things that are unique to each historical moment, it's fascinating to see what happens when historical moments are reanimated and can help shed light on our contemporary moment."

As for protest signs, Walker argued that the shift in context is a little different from their more formal counterparts. "For protest signs there is a primary audience of participants and immediate observers of the protest, and a secondary audience that might see the signs in photographs or video footage after the fact," she explained.

"Particularly in contemporary protests you see a lot of signs that seem to be made with this secondary audience in mind, made to be photographed," she clarified. "There is a lot of engagement with meme culture or rhetoric, likely with the hope of virality."

She was quick to point out that this is not something unique to the era of social media. "It is really interesting, though, that protestors in the 1960s were often similarly media savvy and very aware of optics and using photography to spread their messages to a larger audience," she said. Just as history repeats, then, so too do the signs that accompany it. Could a museum exhibit clarify someone's politics just as easily as a campaign poster or protest signs? The answer is almost certainly yes.

CONCLUSION

When I began outlining this project, one of the things that stuck with me was the variety of scales from which political signage can be perceived: the immediacy of a yard sign; the impersonal scale of a billboard seen from a distance as you pass it on the highway. The tattoo seen on the arm or leg of a pedestrian you pass on the street—or that you see, in reverse, when you look in the mirror. The political sign in a work of art seen on a museum wall, separated by distance and context.

At the beginning, I thought that this was going to be a book about differing scales; a kind of *Powers of Ten*, but for political signage. If that sounds obscure, well, welcome to how my brain works. But what started to come to mind as I looked at the information gathered, the history and the conversations with curators and the exploration of images from bygone decades, was that this book was less about scale and was instead more about communication.

This is a book that begins with yard signs and expands outward from there, following political signage from that initial permutation into a succession of forms and formats.

One of the reasons I began with yard signs is their modesty—yes, their scale—but there's something else at hand here. Yard signs are a thoroughly basic form of political signage. They're a kind of coelacanth, something that reached its ideal form long ago and has contentedly stayed there, not evolving because it didn't need to evolve any further. In Joe McGinniss's *The Selling of the President*, he cited George H. W. Bush's 1966 campaign for a House seat. "Eighty percent of George Bush's campaign budget went to advertising," McGinniss wrote. "Fifty-nine percent of this went to television. Newspapers got three percent."[1] Even so, signage endures.

There's something laudable in that, I think. Alternately: Human-scale political signs existed in American politics before the Eisenhower campaign made its breakthrough decision to work with an advertising agency. That campaign changed the role of political signage in campaigning, but the old forms stuck around—perhaps with a reduced budget, but with a presence nonetheless. And a sense of what a political sign could be is also constantly evolving. In 2013, after Super Typhoon Haiyan struck the Philippines and killed more than 6,000 people, images of disaster relief supplies began to show up on social media. But there was something unique about them: They contained the names of various politicians along with their campaigns' logos.[2] Life-saving supplies as political signs? That's probably not the strangest, or most cynical, example of political signage out there.

*   *   *

While the internet has certainly made it easier for political signage and political advertising to reach people, sometimes to a fault—see also, the 2016 presidential election—this is not a book of the "the internet *changed everything*" vein. What the internet did do was create a place for connections and for the circulation of political signage. Consider the example of Led By Donkeys.

One of the reasons the pussyhat designs associated with the 2017 Women's March were able to spread so quickly was due to the online knitting community Ravelry,[3] for instance. If I want to explore the protest signs of the pro-democracy movement in Hong Kong, that artwork[4] is just a click away. Activists in Hong Kong also developed a striking riff on Inktober, a month-long event in which illustrators post new images each day for the month of October; #freetoberHK presented a spin on this in which illustrators could address the issues raised by protests and the government's crackdown through their own artwork—expanding the protest into the digital realm.

* * *

It's been an education. Perhaps the fourth and final lesson was sitting down and writing this book.

As a believer in the importance of media literacy, I think that studying the past permutations of political signage are useful for comprehending thematic trends and political futures. Consider, perhaps, some unholy combination of John

Berger's *Ways of Seeing* and George Orwell's "Politics and the English Language." By the dual natures of political signage and political science, that very combination might need to be tweaked discreetly for the appropriate regional audience. Or, as Marshall McLuhan writes in his essay "Advertising as a Magical Institution," "Ads are social situations."[5] And most political signs are, at their core, ads.

What's next for political signs? Further breaks from tradition seem like a very real possibility. "Lately, it's been interesting to see how many candidates are veering from the red and blue theme," Christen Carter of the Busy Beaver Button Museum said. That's a bold thing to hear; it offers the potential of new baselines being set and new territory charted. It also suggests that some of the long-standing visual cues viewers associate with certain political entities could fall out of use.

*   *   *

No political sign emerges from a vacuum. Even the most nominally singular of them are in dialogue with what's come before. One can listen for changes, listen for alterations, and listen for the political conversations that can spark changes in the signs that we pass each day. But there's also the importance of seeing, of studying, of understanding what's before us all.

If this book had an epigraph, it would be by John Berger because reading John Berger was critically important for me in understanding the concept of media literacy. That can sound like a foreboding term, but it's not intended as such. Media literary, to me, simply means understanding why something is being broadcast—figuratively or literally—in front of you. And that's something everyone can do. Alternately, as the early punk band The Desperate Bicycles once stated, in a song almost as old as me, "It was easy, it was cheap—go and do it!"[6]

The resources to understand why a political sign exists and what it might be saying—both overtly and subtly—are present in books, journals, and online. There's also the act of detachment: When you see a political sign, what does it remind you of? How would you interpret the words on it, outside of their ideological or partisan context? What do its colors, its location, and its presence meant to you?

Alternately? It can begin with a single act, and that's to take in the sign before you. From there comes consideration; from there might well come revelation. But those modest beginnings are what sparks it all. Alternately, to borrow a few words from the phrase emblazoned on my arm: see; now. What do we have to lose?

ACKNOWLEDGMENTS & THANKS

This book would not have been possible without the assistance and friendship of Scott Shields. Scott was also an invaluable source of information on the role political signage played (and continues to play) in local, state, and national elections.

Tremendous thanks are due to Kristen Marttila for providing the legal context for the Supreme Court verdict referenced herein. Articles written for News-to-Table and Inside Hook also helped me shape some of the ideas found in this book. Many thanks in particular to Jason Diamond, Walker Loetscher, Alexander Zaitchik, and Jeff Koyen.

I am indebted to everyone at Bloomsbury and Object Lessons, especially Haaris Naqvi, Amy Martin, Christopher Schaberg, and Ian Bogost, for their work on this book.

Thanks to Susan Carlson at the International Center of Photography, Melissa Walker at Poster House, Troy Elkins and Kevin M. Bailey at the Dwight D. Eisenhower Presidential Library, Meghan Lee-Parker at the Richard Nixon Presidential

Library and Museum, Michelle M. Frauenberger at the Franklin D. Roosevelt Presidential Library, Dana Howell at the Monmouth County Historical Association, the staff of the Texas State Library and Archives Commission, Christen Carter at the Busy Beaver Button Museum, and Kelsey Halliday Johnson at Space 538. Thanks to Mairead Case and Rachel Knaizer for talking political tattoos with me, Michele Filgate for talking nonfiction structure with me, Jacqueline Mabey for talking art and politics with me, and Duncan B. Barlow for being an excellent tourmate. Tremendous thanks and a raised pint (or Powers shot) to my cohorts at Brooklyn Spurs and Empire Supporters Club. Thanks to Kristen and Charlie Marttila for recommending *Resistance, Protest, Resilience*; without having seen it, this book would be very different. And, as this book's dedication suggests, abundant thanks are also due to my parents for raising me to think critically about politics, advertising, and media.

Much of this book was written while on residencies at Art Farm in Marquette, Nebraska and Fish Factory in Stöðvarfjörður, Iceland. Huge thanks are due to Ed Dadey, Assi Kerttu Sofia, Rósa Valtingojer, Una Sigurðardóttir, and Vincent Wood. Huge thanks are also due to my fellow residents at both, who helped to shape my thinking on this book.

NOTES

Introduction

1 Patrick Gavin, "Romney Campaign's Lasting Mark," POLITICO, November 12, 2012, https://www.politico.com/story/2012/11/so-maybe-that-romney-face-tattoo-wasnt-such-a-good-idea-romneys-campaign-leaves-lasting-impression-083689.

2 Marshall McLuhan, *Understanding Media: The Extensions of Man* (New York: McGraw-Hill, 1964).

3 "Martin Kaplan," The Norman Lear Center, accessed November 13, 2019, https://learcenter.org/kaplan/.

Chapter 1

1 Melissa Febos, "Teaching After Trump," *Granta*, November 16, 2016, https://granta.com/teaching-after-trump/.

Chapter 2

1 Kathleen Jamie, *Sightlines: A Conversation with the Natural World* (New York: The Experiment, LLC, 2013), 46.

2 David Giambusso, "Newark Neighborhood Calls for an End to Campaign Sign 'Litter,'" *Star-Ledger*, March 9, 2014, https://www.nj.com/essex/2014/03/newark_neighborhood_calls_f or_an_end_to_campaign_sign_litter.html.

3 Zach Paterberg, "Passaic sign wars heat up," *The Record*, October 18, 2013.

4 Jessica Mazzola, "Democratic Campaign Worker Charged With Swiping Campaign Signs," Mahwah, NJ *Patch*, October 24, 2012, https://patch.com/new-jersey/mahwah/democrati c-campaign-worker-charged-with-swiping-campaign-signs.

5 Keith Edwards, "Political Signs Upset Apple Orchard Owner," *Kennebec Journal and Morning Sentinel*, October 24, 2012, https://www.centralmaine.com/2012/10/24/political-signs upset-apple-cart_2012-10-23/.

6 Ibid.

7 Lane Wallace, "The Popularity and Irrelevance of Our Lawn Sign Wars," *Atlantic*, November 3, 2012, https://www.theatlan tic.com/national/archive/2012/11/the-popularity-and-irreleva nce-of-our-lawn-sign-wars/264488/.

8 Ibid.

9 Ibid.

10 Eric Lutz, "Teens Face Hate Crime Charges for Burning Trump Campaign Sign," *Business Insider*, April 21, 2017, https://www.businessinsider.com/teens-face-hate-crime-charge s-for-burning-trump-campaign-sign-2017-4?r=US&IR=T.

11 Ibid.

12 "Burning a Trump Sign Is Not a Hate Crime," *Baltimore Sun*, May 31, 2019, https://www.baltimoresun.com/opinion/edi torial/bs-ed-hate-crime-trump-20170419-story.html.

13 Jessica Anderson, "Hate-Crime Charges Dropped against Two Women Accused of Setting Trump Sign on Fire, Police Say," *Baltimore Sun*, June 30, 2019, https://www.baltimoresun.com/news/crime/bs-md-trump-sign-folo-20170420-story.html.

14 "*Reed et al. v. Town of Gilbert, Arizona et al.*," Supreme Court of the United States, accessed November 1, 2019, https://www.supremecourt.gov/opinions/14pdf/13-502_9olb.pdf.

15 Lyle Denniston, "Opinion Analysis: The Message Determines the Right," SCOTUSblog, June 18, 2015, https://www.scotusblog.com/2015/06/opinion-analysis-the-message-determines-the-right/.

Chapter 3

1 Joe McGinniss, *The Selling of the President* (New York: Penguin Books, 1988), 27.

2 Art and Picture Collection, The New York Public Library, "Tammany Hall in its glory—its appearance in the presidential campaign, 1856—reception of the Keystone Club from Philadephia," New York Public Library Digital Collections, accessed October 17, 2019, http://digitalcollections.nypl.org/items/510d47e0-cd2b-a3d9-e040-e00a18064a99.

3 Art and Picture Collection, The New York Public Library, "Presidential electioneering in New York—torchlight procession of the McClellan party," New York Public Library Digital Collections, accessed October 17, 2019, http://digitalcollections.nypl.org/items/510d47e0-cd0f-a3d9-e040-e00a18064a99.

4   "McClellan for President," Charles Magnus, New York, 1864, https://www.loc.gov/item/scsm000501/.

5   "Lincoln and Hamlin! Campaign of !," 1860, https://www.loc.gov/item/scsm000562/.

6   John E. Hollitz, "Eisenhower and the Admen: The Television 'Spot' Campaign of 1952," *Wisconsin Magazine of History* 66, no. 1 (1982): 25–39, http://www.jstor.org/stable/4635688.

7   Yoni Applebaum, "The Man Nobody Knows," *Atlantic*, June 9, 2016, https://www.theatlantic.com/politics/archive/2016/06/the-trump-nobody-knows/486251/.

8   George Dugan, "John Orr Young Is Dead at 89; Co-Founded Young & Rubicam," *New York Times*, May 3, 1976, https://www.nytimes.com/1976/05/03/archives/john-orr-young-is-dead-at-89-cofounded-young-rubicam-briefcase-was.html.

9   David Haven Blake, "The 2016 Campaign and the Lessons of Eisenhower's Birthday," *Time*, accessed October 17, 2019, https://time.com/4525301/ike-day-presidential-entertainment/.

10 Ibid.

11 Marshall McLuhan and Richard Cavell, *On the Nature of Media: Essays, 1952–1978* (Berkeley: Gingko Press, 2016), 95.

12 Eugene Robinson, "CHILE'S PINOCHET BEATEN IN PLEBISCITE ON RULE," *Washington Post*, October 6, 1988, https://www.washingtonpost.com/archive/politics/1988/10/06/chiles-pinochet-beaten-in-plebiscite-on-rule/cbc2e773-f1cc-4c37-bcb5-91b9de1e8084/.

13 Larry Rohter, "One Prism on the Undoing of Pinochet," *New York Times*, accessed October 17, 2019, https://www.nytimes.com/2013/02/10/movies/oscar-nominated-no-stirring-debate-in-chile.html.

14 Emma Hall and Alexandra Jardine, "Brexit Autopsy: How the Ad Battle Played Out (and What the U.S. Should Learn From It)," *AdAge*, June 30, 2016, https://adage.com/article/advertising/brexit-media-battle-u-s-learn/304765.

15 Will Craig, "I Was Part of the Remain Campaign. There Are Lessons in Brexit: The Uncivil War," *The Guardian*, January 8, 2019, https://www.theguardian.com/commentisfree/2019/jan/08/i-was-in-remain-campaign-win-peoples-vote-brexit-the-uncivil-war.

16 Shehab Khan, "The Misinformation That Was Told about Brexit during and after the Referendum," *The Independent*, August 2, 2018, https://www.independent.co.uk/news/uk/politics/final-say-brexit-referendum-lies-boris-johnson-leave-campaign-remain-a8466751.html.

Chapter 4

1 Staff, "Bush Site Unplugs Poster Tool," *Wired*, June 5, 2017, https://www.wired.com/2004/03/bush-site-unplugs-poster-tool/.

2 Ibid.

3 Chris O'Falt, "'Kill All Others': Dee Rees's 'Electric Dreams' Episode Is a Masterclass in Science-fiction World-building," https://www.indiewire.com/2018/06/kill-all-others-dee-rees-electric-dreams-masterclass-science-fiction-1201972356/.

Chapter 5

1 Candy Woodall, "Scott Wagner to Gov. Tom Wolf: 'I'm Going to Stomp All over Your Face with Golf Spikes,'" *York Daily*

Record, October 15, 2018, https://eu.ydr.com/story/news/polit
ics/elections/2018/10/12/pa-election-governor-race-scott-wag
ner-says-hell-stomp-all-over-gov-tom-wolf-face-golf-spikes-v
ideo/1613872002/.

2 Jan Murphy, "Scott Wagner's 'Strong Arm' Collection Tactics
Are Focus of Rt. 581 Billboard," PennLive, September 14, 2018,
https://www.pennlive.com/politics/2018/09/group_takes_a
im_at_gop_guberna.html.

3 Op-Ed, "We're behind the Billboard That Prompted Scott
Wagner's Rant. He's Not Fit to Be Governor: Opinion,"
PennLive, October 13, 2018, https://www.pennlive.com/opini
on/2018/10/we_posted_the_billboard_that_p.html.

4 Jonathan Mahler, "For Mario Cuomo, Defeat in 1977
Mayor's Race Cast a Long Shadow," *New York Times*, January
5, 2015, https://www.nytimes.com/2015/01/05/nyregion/f
or-mario-cuomo-defeat-in-1977-mayors-race-cast-a-long-s
hadow.html.

5 "The Article That Made Mario Cuomo Governor in 1982—No
Kidding!" *Village Voice*, accessed November 13, 2019, https://
www.villagevoice.com/2015/01/06/the-article-that-made-mar
io-cuomo-governor-in-1982-no-kidding/.

6 "About," Stonewall Democratic Club of NYC, accessed
November 13, 2019, http://sdnyc.org/about1.

7 Patrick D. Healy, "Democratic Elbows Are Flying, Mostly
Aimed at Cuomo," *New York Times*, January 27, 2006, https://
www.nytimes.com/2006/01/27/nyregion/democratic-elbow
s-are-flying-mostly-aimed-at-cuomo.html.

8 Michael Barbaro, "Doubts About Cuomo's Support of Gay
Rights," *New York Times*, July 8, 2010, https://www.nytimes.
com/2010/07/09/nyregion/09gays.html.

9   Elizabeth Kolbert, "Postscript: Mario Cuomo (1932–2015),"
    New Yorker, June 20, 2017, https://www.newyorker.com/news/
    news-desk/postscript-mario-cuomo.

Chapter 6

1   Stephen King, *11/22/63* (New York: Scribner, 2011), 296.

2   Frank Rich, "Frank Rich: How Obama's Presidency Mirrors
    JFK's," *New York Magazine*, November 18, 2011, http://nym
    ag.com/news/frank-rich/jfk-2011-11/.

3   Stephen King, *The Outsider: A Novel* (New York: Scribner,
    2018), 305.

4   King, *The Outsider*, 360.

5   "Saatchi & Saatchi: The Agency That Made Tory History,"
    The Independent, September 18, 2011, https://www.independ
    ent.co.uk/news/media/saatchi-saatchi-the-agency-that-ma
    de-tory-history-744791.html.

6   Sam Delaney, "The 10 Best British Political Posters,"
    The Guardian, April 3, 2015, https://www.theguardian.com/ar
    tanddesign/2015/apr/03/the-10-best-british-political-posters.

7   Martyn Walsh, "My Campaign: The Creation of the 'Labour
    Isn't Working' Poster of 1978," CampaignUK, October 25,
    2018, https://www.campaignlive.co.uk/article/campaign-cr
    eation-labour-isnt-working-poster-1978/1496488.

8   Ibid.

9   Richard Hamilton, *Kent State*, 1970, TateUK, accessed
    November 14, 2019, https://www.tate.org.uk/art/artworks/
    hamilton-kent-state-p77043.

10 Heather Stewart and Rowena Mason, "Nigel Farage's Anti-Migrant Poster Reported to Police," *The Guardian*, June 16, 2016, https://www.theguardian.com/politics/2016/jun/16/nigel-farage-defends-ukip-breaking-point-poster-queue-of-migrants.

11 Ibid.

12 Led By Donkeys, "Boris Johnson Brutally Trolled on Huge Billboard in Birmingham," *Birmingham Mail*, October 1, 2019, https://www.birminghammail.co.uk/news/midlands-news/boris-johnson-brutally-trolled-huge-17013382.

13 "The Brexit Party Manifesto," accessed November 14, 2019, https://thebrexitparty.com/.

14 Ben Quinn, "Get Ready for Brexit Satire: Led By Donkeys Launches Billboard Contest," *The Guardian*, September 25, 2019, https://www.theguardian.com/politics/2019/sep/25/get-ready-for-brexit-satire-led-by-donkeys-launches-billboard-contest.

15 Ben Quinn, "Brexit the Horror Film: Billboards Mock Government's 'Get Ready' Campaign," *The Guardian*, October 12, 2019, https://www.theguardian.com/politics/2019/oct/12/brexit-the-horror-film-billboards-mock-governments-get-ready-campaign-led-by-donkeys.

16 Led By Donkeys, "We're Led by Donkeys (Location: Cheltenham, Feb '19) Pic.twitter.com/bj25PrXcU8," Twitter, October 8, 2019, https://twitter.com/ByDonkeys/status/1181534389395697664.

17 Led By Donkeys, "Boris Johnson Sold Us Brexit by Pretending to Care about the Sovereignty of Our Parliament. Now He Wants to Suspend Parliament to Further His Career. This Country Didn't Elect Him. He Must Be Stopped. Pic.twitter.com/plGlJ2Rr0Q," Twitter, August 28, 2019, https://twitter.com/ByDonkeys/status/1166657270148665344.

18 Chiara Giordano, "Trump Faces Giant Projections on London Landmarks during State Visit," *The Independent*, June 3, 2019, https://www.independent.co.uk/news/uk/home-news/tr ump-protest-uk-obama-approval-ratings-john-mccain-led-b y-donkeys-a8942156.html.

Chapter 8

1 Olivia Laing, "David Wojnarowicz: Still Fighting Prejudice 24 Years after His Death," *The Guardian*, May 12, 2016, https://www.theguardian.com/books/2016/may/13/david-wojnarow icz-close-to-the-knives-a-memoir-of-disintegration-artist-ai ds-activist.

2 Ibid.

3 Amy Oringel, "The Secret Jewish History Of The Pussyhat," *Forward*, March 7, 2017, https://forward.com/culture/365099/ the-secret-jewish-history-of-the-pussyhat/.

4 Ibid.

5 DeNeen L. Brown, "'I Am a Man': The Ugly Memphis Sanitation Workers' Strike That Led to MLK's Assassination," *Washington Post*, July 31, 2019, https://www.washingtonpost.com/news/retr opolis/wp/2018/02/12/i-am-a-man-the-1968-memphis-sanita tion-workers-strike-that-led-to-mlks-assassination/.

6 "Sheehan Resumes Protest Vigil," CNN, August 25, 2005, http://us.cnn.com/2005/POLITICS/08/25/crawford.protest/index .html.

7 Melanie Markley and Houston Chronicle, "Bush Has Teleconference before Return to Washington," *Houston Chronicle*, July 30, 2011, https://www.chron.com/news/hur

ricanes/article/Bush-has-teleconference-before-return-to-166
3189.php.

8 Getty, "Vietnam War Protest," ABC News, May 3, 2019, Getty
   Images, https://www.abc.net.au/news/2019-05-03/vietna
   m-war-protest/11078410.

9 Marina Koren, "A Brief History of Die-In Protests," CityLab,
   December 4, 2014, https://www.citylab.com/equity/2014/12/a
   -brief-history-of-die-in-protests/383439/.

10 Ray Filar, "Silence = Death: Sarah Schulman on ACT UP, the
   Forgotten Resistance to the AIDS Crisis," openDemocracy,
   January 30, 2014, https://www.opendemocracy.net/en/transfo
   rmation/silence-death-sarah-schulman-on-act-up-forgotte
   n-resistance-to-aids-crisis/.

11 Katie Zezima, "Students Stage 'Die-Ins' Nationwide to Protest
   Gun Violence," *Washington Post*, June 13, 2018, https://ww
   w.washingtonpost.com/national/2018/06/12/students-stage
   -die-ins-nationwide-to-protest-gun-violence/.

12 Didi Kirsten Tatlow, "In Villages, Praying for the Souls of
   Tibetan Self-Immolators," *New York Times*, February 3, 2013,
   https://rendezvous.blogs.nytimes.com/2013/02/03/in-villages-
   praying-for-the-souls-of-tibetan-self-immolaters/.

13 "South Viet Nam: The Light That Failed," *Time*, June 10, 1966,
   http://content.time.com/time/subscriber/article/0,33009,9420
   06,00.html.

Chapter 9

1 Jack Bell, "F.C. New York Likes Mitt," *New York Times*, June
   30, 2012, https://goal.blogs.nytimes.com/2012/06/30/f-c-new-
   york-likes-mitt/.

2 Ibid.

3 Sean Lengell, "Romney Donor Gets Boot in Soccer Deal," *Washington Times*, July 3, 2012, https://www.washingtontim es.com/news/2012/jul/3/romney-donor-gets-boot-in-soccer -deal/.

4 Dave Levinthal, "Conservative Group's NASCAR Drive," POLITICO, February 9, 2012, https://www.politico.com/story /2012/02/conservative-group-makes-nascar-ad-buy-072667.

5 "About American Majority," American Majority, September 5, 2019, https://www.americanmajority.org/about/.

6 Levinthal, "Conservative Group's NASCAR Drive."

7 Lorena Arroyo, "Brazilian Football Club Celebrates Che Guevara Link," BBC News, December 31, 2013, https://ww w.bbc.com/news/world-latin-america-25489007.

8 "2013 Madureira 'Che Guevara 50 Years' Shirts," Vintage Football Shirts, accessed November 14, 2019, https://www.vin tagefootballshirts.com/blog/2013-madureira-che-guevara-50- years-shirts/8.

9 Ibid.

10 Arroyo, "Brazilian Football Club Celebrates Che Guevara Link."

11 Ibid.

12 Catherine E. Shoichet, Julian Cummings, and Holly Yan, "LeBron James and Other NBA Players Don 'I Can't Breathe' Shirts," CNN, December 9, 2014, http://us.cnn.com/2014/12 /08/justice/protests-grand-jury-chokehold/index.html.

13 Nick Schwartz, "10 Times LeBron James Stood up to Donald Trump," *USA Today*, August 5, 2018, https://ftw.usatoday .com/2018/08/10-times-lebron-james-stood-up-to-donald-t rump.

14 Neil Vigdor, "Stephon Clark's Sons Reach $2.4 Million Settlement Over Police Killing," *New York Times*, October 11, 2019, https://www.nytimes.com/2019/10/10/us/stephon-clark-shooting-settlement.html.

15 Sharon Bernstein, "NBA's Kings and Celtics Protest Police Shootings of Unarmed Black Men," Reuters, March 26, 2018, https://www.reuters.com/article/us-california-police-kings/nbas-kings-and-celtics-protest-police-shootings-of-unarmed-black-men-idUSKBN1H201P.

16 Ibid.

17 Christina Cauterucci, "The WNBA's Black Lives Matter Protest Has Set a New Standard for Sports Activism," Slate, July 25, 2016, https://slate.com/human-interest/2016/07/the-wnbas-black-lives-matter-protest-has-set-new-standard-for-sports-activism.html.

18 Ibid.

19 Ibid.

Chapter 10

1 Richard Ballout, "Why Everything You Know about the Madrid Derby Might Be Wrong," FourFourTwo, June 26, 2015, https://www.fourfourtwo.com/features/why-everything-you-know-about-madrid-derby-might-be-wrong.

2 "UEFA Charges Polish Club over Warsaw Uprising Tifo," DailySabah, www.dailysabah.com, August 4, 2017, https://www.dailysabah.com/football/2017/08/04/uefa-charges-polish-club-over-warsaw-uprising-tifo.

3 "Legia Warsaw Supporters Hit out at UEFA with Giant Banner of a Pig," *Daily Mirror*, August 18, 2017, https://www.mirror.co.uk/sport/football/news/legia-warsaw-supporters-hit-out-11008609.

4 Kim McCauley, "MLS Can Only Blame Itself for the Backlash against Its Politics Ban," SBNation.com, August 24, 2019, https://www.sbnation.com/soccer/2019/8/23/20830033/mls-political-sign-ban-timbers-sounders-protest-antifa.

5 Jeff Rueter, "USL Takes a Hands-off Approach to Political Speech from Its...," The Athletic, October 9, 2019, https://theathletic.com/1280822/2019/10/09/.

6 Leander Schaerlaeckens, "The Socialist Soccer Fans Who Saved MLS From Neo-Nazis," Vice, November 29, 2015, https://www.vice.com/en_us/article/bmqgxv/the-socialist-soccer-fans-who-saved-mls-from-neo-nazis.

7 James F. Clarity and Warren Weaver, "Of John 3:16," *New York Times*, November 27, 1985, https://www.nytimes.com/1985/11/27/us/briefing-of-john-3-16.html.

8 "The Unbelievable Life of the 'John 3:16' Sports Guy," Mental Floss, August 18, 2017, https://mentalfloss.com/article/500515/unbelievable-life-john-316-sports-guy.

9 Clarity and Weaver, "Of John 3:16."

10 "Cheap Seats Daily: Will 'Dumb' and 'Dumber' Shirts Be Allowed at Snyder's 'Night of Quarterbacks'?" *Washington City Paper*, accessed November 13, 2019, https://www.washingtoncitypaper.com/news/city-desk/blog/13059924/cheap-seats-daily-will-dumb-and-dumber-shirts-be-allowed-at-snyders-night-of-quarterbacks.

11 Monte Burke, "The Resurrection of John 3:16," *Forbes*, July 11, 2012, https://www.forbes.com/2009/11/12/john-316-sign-lifestyle-sports-rainbow-man.html#16ee6b475e3a.

12 Andy Barr, "Abortion Groups Tangle over Tebow," POLITICO, January 27, 2010, https://www.politico.com/story/2010/01/a bortion-groups-tangle-over-tebow-032052.

13 Rob Tornoe, "Tim Tebow to Donald Trump: Thanks, but No Thanks," *Philadelphia Inquirer*, July 14, 2016, https://www.inq uirer.com/philly/blogs/real-time/Tim-Tebow-to-speak-dur ing-Donald-Trumps-Republican-National-Convention.html.

14 Wrap Staff, "'Run the Race' Film Review: Tim Tebow's Faith-Based Football Saga Elevates the Material a Step or Two," TheWrap, February 23, 2019, https://www.thewrap.com/r un-the-race-film-review-tim-tebow/.

15 Electa Draper, "Focus on the Family Unveils John 3:16 Ad during Broncos Game," *Denver Post*, June 23, 2017, https://ww w.denverpost.com/2012/01/14/focus-on-the-family-unveils -john-316-ad-during-broncos-game-2/.

16 Ibid.

17 Adam Ericksen, "How Progressive Christians Can Reclaim John 3:16," Patheos, March 12, 2018, https://www.patheos. com/blogs/teachingnonviolentatonement/2018/03/progressi ve-christians-can-reclaim-john-316/.

Interlude: The Punk Chapter

1 Travis Andrews, "Behind the Right's Loathing of the NEA: Two 'Despicable' Exhibits Almost 30 Years Ago," *Washington Post*, April 29, 2019, https://www.washingtonpost.com/news/morn ing-mix/wp/2017/03/20/behind-the-loathing-of-the-nation al-endowment-for-the-arts-a-pair-of-despicable-exhibits-almo st-30-years-ago/.

2 Bernard Weinraub, "Filmmakers Discount Criticism by Dole," *New York Times*, June 2, 1995, https://www.nytimes.com/1 995/06/02/us/filmmakers-discount-criticism-by-dole.html.

3 Benjamin Nugent, "Why Don't Republicans Write Fiction?" *n + 1*, March 6, 2014, https://nplusonemag.com/online-only/ online-only/why-dont-republicans-write-fiction/.

Chapter 11

1 Jeffrey Toobin, "The Dirty Trickster," *New Yorker*, January 25, 2019, https://www.newyorker.com/magazine/2008/06/02/the-dirty-trickster.

2 Luke Lewis, "This Guy Has A Margaret Thatcher Tattoo," BuzzFeed, April 17, 2013, https://www.buzzfeed.com/lukel ewis/this-guy-has-a-margaret-thatcher-tattoo.

3 Katy Docherty, "Maggie Mourner's Skull and Crossbones Tattoo Dedication: 'She Never Turned'," *The Sun*, April 5, 2016, https://www.thesun.co.uk/archives/news/672394/magg ie-mourners-tattoo-tribute-she-never-turned/.

4 Sarah Rogers, "The Shop That Spawned 78 Trump Tattoos," *Daily Beast*, May 26, 2018, https://www.thedailybeast.com/ the-shop-that-spawned-78-trump-tattoos.

5 Ibid.

6 Ibid.

7 Kurt Halsey, "Ralph Nader Tattoo," Flickr, October 9, 2008, https://www.flickr.com/photos/swiftscout4/2925602785.

8 John Hind, "Did I Say That? Diego Maradona, Football Coach, 49," *The Guardian*, November 22, 2009, https://www.

theguardian.com/football/2009/nov/22/diego-maradona-d
id-i-say-that.

9   "Maradona Wants Tattoo of Chavez," Reuters, December 13,
    2007, https://www.reuters.com/article/us-chavez/maradona
    -wants-tattoo-of-chavez-idUSN1365093020071213.

10 Joe Gorman, "Great Sporting-Political Friendships,"
    The Guardian, September 10, 2013, https://www.theguardian.
    com/sport/blog/2013/sep/10/great-sporting-friendships-po
    liticians-maradona-castro.

11 Darryn Albert, "John Wall Got Black Power Fist Tattoo,"
    Larry Brown Sports, October 2, 2017, https://larrybrownsp
    orts.com/basketball/john-wall-black-power-fist-tattoo/
    399506.

12 Ariela Gittlen, "This Artist Built a Tattoo Parlor Dedicated to
    Black Pride," Artsy, February 1, 2018, https://www.artsy.net/
    article/artsy-editorial-artist-built-tattoo-parlor-dedicated-bl
    ack-pride.

13 Grant Morrison, *The Invisibles: The Invisible Kingdom* (New
    York: DC Comics, 2002).

Chapter 12

1   "Barack Obama's Remarks to the Democratic National
    Convention," *New York Times*, July 27, 2004, https://www.nyt
    imes.com/2004/07/27/politics/campaign/barack-obamas-rem
    arks-to-the-democratic-national.html.

2   David Balzer, *Curationism: How Curating Took Over the Art
    World and Everything Else* (Toronto: Coach House Books,
    2015), 8–9.

3 Steven Heller, "A Design Challenge: What If Nixon, Lincoln, or Bush Were Running Again?" *Atlantic*, May 11, 2012, https://www.theatlantic.com/entertainment/archive/2012/05/a-design-challenge-what-if-nixon-lincoln-or-bush-were-running-again/256978/.

4 "ReElect: Gerald Ford," Jennifer Rozbruch Design, accessed November 13, 2019, https://jennyrozbruch.com/reelect-gerald-ford.

5 Steven Heller, "Could Washington, Lincoln or Taft Be Elected Today?" *Print*, April 9, 2013, https://www.printmag.com/imprint/could-washington-lincoln-or-taft-be-elected-today/.

6 Sarah Moss, *Names for the Sea: Strangers in Iceland* (Berkeley: Counterpoint, 2013), 138.

7 "Tony Puryear," Tony Puryear, accessed November 13, 2019, https://www.tonypuryear.com/#/hillary-2-1/.

8 Bryan Adams, *Hillary Clinton*, National Portrait Gallery, accessed November 13, 2019, https://npg.si.edu/object/npg_NPG.2011.123.

9 Justin Worland, "Shepard Fairey: Artist Endorses Bernie Sanders With Shirt," *Time*, February 18, 2016, https://time.com/4229162/shepard-fairey-bernie-sanders/.

10 "Obama 'Hope' Artist's Take on Donald Trump," CNN, November 8, 2016, https://edition.cnn.com/style/article/shepard-fairey-interview/index.html.

11 " Demagogue," Franz Ferdinand, 30 Days, 30 Songs, accessed November 13, 2019, http://www.30days30songs.com/5.

12 "Obama 'Hope' Artist's Take on Donald Trump."

13 "Contradiction—Robbie Conal: The Broad," Robbie Conal | The Broad, accessed November 13, 2019, https://www.thebroad.org/art/robbie-conal/contradiction.

14 Marc Fisher, "A FAST-PASTE NIGHT OF PROTEST ACTIVIST-ARTIST ROBBIE CONAL AND HIS LATEST CREW POSTER THE TOWN," *Washington Post*, May 22, 1995, https://www.washingtonpost.com/archive/lifestyle/1995/05/22/a-fast-paste-night-of-protest-activist-artist-robbie-conal-and-his-latest-crew-poster-the-town/2ec6ee42-fb77-4eaf-b389-61de756f8147/.

15 Victoria Looseleaf, "Robbie Conal," Art Now LA, October 8, 2018, https://artnowla.com/2018/10/07/robbie-conal/.

16 Rory Carroll, "'I Think Leftism Is a Disorder': Is This Artist the Rightwing Banksy?" *The Guardian*, June 21, 2017, https://www.theguardian.com/artanddesign/2017/jun/21/rightwing-street-artist-sabo-donald-trump-la.

17 Katie Zezima, "The Guy Who Made Ted Cruz into a Ripped, Tattooed Smoker," *Washington Post*, May 1, 2019, https://www.washingtonpost.com/news/post-politics/wp/2015/02/27/the-guy-who-made-ted-cruz-into-a-ripped-tattooed-smoker/.

18 Deena Zaru, "Sabo's Journey from #NeverTrump, to the Trump Train," CNN, August 16, 2017, https://edition.cnn.com/2016/11/08/politics/sabo-conservative-artist-gets-political/index.html.

19 Carroll, "'I Think Leftism Is a Disorder': Is This Artist the Rightwing Banksy?"

20 Zezima, "The Guy Who Made Ted Cruz into a Ripped, Tattooed Smoker."

21 Zaru, "Sabo's Journey from #NeverTrump, to the Trump Train."

22 Zezima, "The Guy Who Made Ted Cruz into a Ripped, Tattooed Smoker."

23 Carroll, "'I Think Leftism Is a Disorder': Is This Artist the Rightwing Banksy?"

Chapter 13

1   Ulysses S. Grant 1872 campaign poster, iowaculture.gov, accessed November 13, 2019, https://iowaculture.gov/history/education/educator-resources/primary-source-sets/caucuses-and-elections/ulysses-s-grant.

2   "Mondale-Ferraro Campaign Poster," Bullock, Texas State History Museum, accessed November 13, 2019, https://www.thestoryoftexas.com/discover/artifacts/artifact-spolight-mondale-ferraro-campaign-poster.

3   "Warhol's Pop Politics," Smithsonian.com, October 30, 2008, https://www.smithsonianmag.com/arts-culture/warhols-pop-politics-89185734/.

4   "Vote McGovern 84— Andy Warhol," Revolver Gallery, accessed November 13, 2019, https://revolverwarholgallery.com/portfolio/vote-mcgovern-fs-ii84/.

5   Andy Warhol and Pat Hackett, *The Andy Warhol Diaries* (New York: Twelve, 2014), via Google Books, no page number given.

6   Aja Romano, "Review: Scary Stories to Tell in the Dark Needs More Scary Stories," Vox, August 9, 2019, https://www.vox.com/culture/2019/8/9/20791547/review-scary-stories-to-tell-in-the-dark-vietnam.

7   James Grebey, "Richard Nixon and Vietnam Are Scary Stories to Tell in the Dark's Strangest Monsters," SYFY WIRE, August 13, 2019, https://www.syfy.com/syfywire/richard-nixon-and-vietnam-are-scary-stories-to-tell-in-the-darks-strangest-monsters.

8   Ken Chen, "The Devil You Know," The New Inquiry, April 18, 2017, https://thenewinquiry.com/the-devil-you-know/.

9   Ibid.

10 Ibid.

11 "Sifting Through the Ashes: Analyzing *Hellblazer*, Part 2," Sequart Organization, accessed November 13, 2019, http://seq uart.org/magazine/51400/analyzing-hellblazer-part-2/.

12 Ed Brubaker and Luke Ross, *Captain America: Two Americas* (New York: Marvel Comics, 2010).

13 Heidi MacDonald, "Tea Party Protests Unintended CAPTAIN AMERICA Portrayal," The Beat, February 10, 2010, https:// www.comicsbeat.com/tea-party-protests-unitended-captain-a merica-portrayal/.

14 Ibid.

15 Kevin Melrose, "Quesada Responds as Captain America's Tea Party Controversy Gains Steam," CBR, February 10, 2010, https://www.cbr.com/quesada-responds-as-captain-america s-tea-party-controversy-gains-steam/.

Chapter 14

1   *Resistance, Protest, Resilience*, Minneapolis Institute of Art, accessed November 13, 2019, https://new.artsmia.org/exhibi tion/resistance-protest-resilience/.

2   Jan-Lodewijk Grootaers, "The art of dissent: How Mia's 'Resistance, Protest, Resilience' photography exhibition came together," Minneapolis Institute of Art, accessed November 13, 2019, https://new.artsmia.org/stories/the-art-of-dissent -how-mias-resistance-protest-resilience-photography-exhibiti on-came-together/.

3   Ibid.

4   Jenna Ross, "Philando Castile Exhibit at Minneapolis Institute
    of Art Embraces Beauty and Trauma," *Star Tribune*, June 19,
    2018, http://www.startribune.com/minneapolis-biggest-mus
    eum-worked-to-get-it-right-with-philando-castile-exhibi
    t/485751391/?refresh=true.

5   Ibid.

6   "A Time to Break Silence: Pictures of Social Change
    Exhibition Opens at Michener Art Museum on September
    9," James A. Michener Art Museum, September 7, 2017, https
    ://www.michenerartmuseum.org/article/8508/a-time-to-bre
    ak-silence-release/.

7   Ibid.

8   Seph Rodney, "An Artist Invites Visitors to Remake Historical
    Protest Signs," Hyperallergic, September 6, 2017, https://hy
    perallergic.com/398173/jason-lazarus-harlem-protest-signs/.

9   "Jason Lazarus," Frieze, accessed November 13, 2019, https://
    frieze.com/article/jason-lazarus.

10 Jason Lazarus, "Jason Lazarus / A Century of Dissent:
    Harlem," Jason Lazarus, accessed November 13, 2019, https://
    jasonlazarus.com/projects/a-century-of-dissent-harlem/.

11 Jason Lazarus, "Jason Lazarus / A Century of Dissent: Miami,"
    Jason Lazarus, accessed November 13, 2019, https://jasonla
    zarus.com/projects/a-century-of-dissent-miami/.

12 Aruna D'Souza, Parker Bright, and Pastiche Lumumba,
    Whitewalling: Art, Race & Protest in 3 Acts (New York:
    Badlands Unlimited, 2018), 29–31.

13 Calvin Tomkins, "Why Dana Schutz Painted Emmett Till,"
    New Yorker, July 9, 2019, https://www.newyorker.com/maga
    zine/2017/04/10/why-dana-schutz-painted-emmett-till.

Conclusion

1 Joe McGinniss, *The Selling of the President* (New York: Penguin Books, 1988), 45.

2 Christina Zdanowicz and Katie Hunt, "Are Philippine Politicians Using Typhoon Aid to Their Advantage?" CNN, November 22, 2013, https://www.cnn.com/2013/11/22/world/asia/philippines-politicians-typhoon-aid-advantage-irpt/index.html.

3 Rosalie Chan, "Ravelry, a Social Network for Knitters with 8 Million Members, Banned Users from Showing Support for Donald Trump on the Platform," Business Insider, June 23, 2019, https://www.businessinsider.com/ravelry-bans-support-donald-trump-knitters-2019-6?r=US&IR=T.

4 Mike Ives and Lam Yik Fei, "At Hong Kong Protests, Art That Imitates Life," *New York Times*, October 11, 2019, https://www.nytimes.com/2019/10/11/world/asia/hong-kong-protest-art.html.

5 Marshall McLuhan and Richard Cavell, *On the Nature of Media: Essays, 1952–1978* (Berkeley: Gingko Press, 2016), 17.

6 The Desperate Bicycles, "Handlebars," from "Smokescreen/Handlebars" seven-inch single, Refill Records, vinyl.

INDEX

OBJECT LESSONS

Cross them all off your list.

exit
LAURA WADDELL
BLOOMSBURY

9781501358159

gin
SHONNA MILLIKEN HUMPHREY
BLOOMSBURY

9781501353277

snake
ERICA WRIGHT
BLOOMSBURY

9781501348716

bulletproof vest
KENNETH R. ROSEN
BLOOMSBURY

9781501353024

coffee
DINAH LENNEY
BLOOMSBURY

9781501344350

environment
ROLF HALDEN
BLOOMSBURY

9781501361906

"Perfect for slipping in a pocket and pulling out when life is on hold."

— Toronto Star

9781501353352

9781501348815

9781501348518

9781501348631

9781501325991

9781501307409

Burger by Carol J. Adams

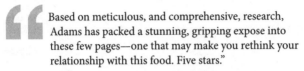

Based on meticulous, and comprehensive, research,
Adams has packed a stunning, gripping expose into
these few pages—one that may make you rethink your
relationship with this food. Five stars."

San Francisco Book Review

Adams would seem the least likely person to write about
hamburgers with her philosophically lurid antipathy to
carnivory. But if the point is to deconstruct this iconic
all-American meal, then she is the woman for the job."

Times Higher Education

It's tempting to say that *Burger* is a literary meal that
fills the reader's need, but that's the essence of Adams'
quick, concise, rich exploration of the role this meat (or
meatless) patty has played in our lives."

PopMatters

High Heel by Summer Brennan

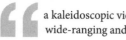

a kaleidoscopic view of feminine public existence, both
wide-ranging and thoughtful."

Jezebel

Brennan makes the case that high heels are an apt
metaphor for the ways in which women have been
hobbled in their mobility. She also tackles the
relationship between beauty and suffering, highlighting
the fraught nature of reclaiming objects defined under
patriarchy for feminism."

Paste Magazine

From Cinderella's glass slippers to Carrie Bradshaw's
Manolo Blahniks, Summer Brennan deftly analyzes
one of the world's most provocative and sexualized
fashion accessories . . . Whether you see high heels
as empowering or a submission to patriarchal gender
roles (or land somewhere in between), you'll likely
never look at a pair the same way again after reading
High Heel."

Longreads

Brennan's book, written in very small sections, is short, but powerful enough to completely change your world view."

Refinery29

In *High Heel*, the wonderful Summer Brennan embraces a slippery, electric conundrum: Does the high heel stand for oppression or power? . . . *High Heel* elevates us, keeps us off balance, and sharpens the point."

The Philadelphia Inquirer

Hood by Alison Kinney

Provocative and highly informative, Alison Kinney's *Hood* considers this seemingly neutral garment accessory and reveals it to be vexed by a long history of violence, from the Grim Reaper to the KKK and beyond—a history we would do well to address, and redress. Readers will never see hoods the same way again."

Sister Helen Prejean, author of
Dead Man Walking

Hood is searing. It describes the historical properties of the hood, but focuses on this object's modern-day connotations. Notably, it dissects the racial fear evoked by young black men in hoodies, as shown by the senseless killings of unarmed black males. It also touches on U.S. service members' use of hoods to mock and torture prisoners at Abu Ghraib. Hoods can represent the (sometimes toxic) power of secret affiliations, from monks to Ku Klux Klan members. And clearly they can also be used by those in power to dehumanize others. In short, *Hood* does an excellent job of unspooling the many faces of hoods."

Book Riot

[*Hood*] is part of a series entitled Object Lessons, which looks at 'the hidden lives of ordinary things' and which are all utterly 'Fridge Brilliant' (defined by TV Tropes as an experience of sudden revelation, like the light coming on when you open a refrigerator door). . . . In many ways *Hood* isn't about hoods at all. It's about what—and who—is under the hood. It's about the hooding, the hooders and the hoodees . . . [and] identity, power and politics. . . . Kinney's book certainly reveals the complex history of the hood in America."

London Review of Books

Personal Stereo by
Rebecca Tuhus-Dubrow

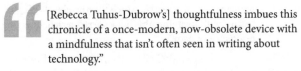

[Rebecca Tuhus-Dubrow's] thoughtfulness imbues this chronicle of a once-modern, now-obsolete device with a mindfulness that isn't often seen in writing about technology."

Pitchfork (named one of *Pitchfork*'s favorite books of 2017)

After finishing *Personal Stereo*, I found myself wondering about the secret lives of every object around me, as if each device were whispering, 'Oh, I am much so more than meets the eye' . . . Tuhus-Dubrow is a master researcher and synthesizer. . . . *Personal Stereo* is a joy to read."

Los Angeles Review of Books

Personal Stereo is loving, wise, and exuberant, a moving meditation on nostalgia and obsolescence. Rebecca Tuhus-Dubrow writes as beautifully about Georg Simmel and Allan Bloom as she does about Jane Fonda and Metallica. Now I understand why I still own the taxicab-yellow Walkman my grandmother gave me in 1988."

Nathaniel Rich, author of
Odds Against Tomorrow

[A] careful, astute study."

The Wire

Souvenir **by Rolf Potts**

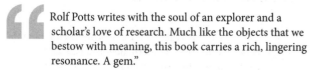

Rolf Potts writes with the soul of an explorer and a scholar's love of research. Much like the objects that we bestow with meaning, this book carries a rich, lingering resonance. A gem."

Andrew McCarthy, actor, director, and author of
The Longest Way Home (2013)

Souvenir, a sweet new book by Rolf Potts, is a little gem (easily tucked into a jacket pocket) filled with big insights . . . *Souvenir* explores our passions for such possessions and why we are compelled to transport items from one spot to another."

Forbes

A treasure trove of . . . fascinating deep dives into the history of travel keepsakes . . . Potts walks us through the origins of some of the most popular vacation memorabilia, including postcards and the still confoundedly ubiquitous souvenir spoons. He also examines the history of the more somber side of mementos, those depicting crimes and tragedies. Overall, the book, as do souvenirs themselves, speaks to the broader issues of time, memory, adventure, and nostalgia."

The Boston Globe

Veil by Rafia Zakaria

"Slim but formidable."

London Review of Books

"Rafia Zakaria's *Veil* shifts the balance away from white
secular Europe toward the experience of Muslim
women, mapping the stereotypical representations of
the veil in Western culture and then reflecting, in an
intensely personal way, on the many meanings that
the veil can have for the people who wear it . . . [*Veil*
is] useful and important, providing needed insight
and detail to deepen our understanding of how we got
here—a necessary step for thinking about whether and
how we might be able to move to a better place."

The Nation

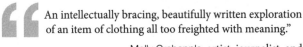

"An intellectually bracing, beautifully written exploration
of an item of clothing all too freighted with meaning."

Molly Crabapple, artist, journalist, and
author of *Drawing Blood* (2015)